Praise for *Black History Is for Everyone*

"Amid widespread political censorship and attacks, *Black History Is for Everyone* pulses with love, insight, and possibility. Brian Jones shares how Black history has challenged and energized his own thinking, inviting each of us to reflect on what we learn, why we learn it, and how it shapes our understanding of the nation and our place in the world. From Bacon's Rebellion to the Haitian Revolution, this book reveals how those who came before us resisted oppression—and reminds us that study and struggle have always gone hand in hand."

—**Ruha Benjamin**, author of *Imagination: A Manifesto*

"With searing honesty and incisive prose, *Black History Is for Everyone* offers a sweeping journey through more than three centuries of Black history. Brian Jones masterfully blends personal reflection with powerful storytelling, revealing the centrality of Black history to American life. Urgent, eye-opening, and deeply engaging, this is essential reading for students, educators, and anyone ready to see the past—and the present—with fresh eyes."

—**Ashley D. Farmer**, author of *Queen Mother: Black Nationalism, Reparations, and the Untold Story of Audley Moore*

BLACK HISTORY IS FOR EVERYONE

Brian Jones

Haymarket Books
Chicago, IL

© 2025 Brian Jones

Published in 2025 by
Haymarket Books
P.O. Box 180165
Chicago, IL 60618
www.haymarketbooks.org

ISBN: 979-8-88890-447-3

Distributed to the trade in the US through Consortium Book Sales and
Distribution (www.cbsd.com) and internationally through Ingram Publisher Services International (www.ingramcontent.com).

This book was published with the generous support of Lannan Foundation,
Wallace Action Fund, and the Marguerite Casey Foundation.

Special discounts are available for bulk purchases by organizations and institutions. Please email info@haymarketbooks.org for more information.

Cover design by Jon Key.

Printed in Canada by union labor.

Library of Congress Cataloging-in-Publication data is available.
Library of Congress Control Number: 2025938365

10 9 8 7 6 5 4 3 2 1

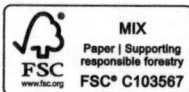
MIX
Paper | Supporting
responsible forestry
FSC
www.fsc.org   FSC® C103567

I went to the 135th Street library at least three or four times a week, and I read everything there. I mean, every single book in that library. In some blind and instinctive way, I knew that what was happening in those books was also happening all around me. And I was trying to make a connection between the books and the life I saw and the life I lived.

—James Baldwin

Contents

Introduction
"Gruesome, Truthful, Yet Digestible"   1

1
Race
Free People of Color   15

2
Nation
"Your National Greatness"   45

3
Revolution
Tout Moun Se Moun   81

4
Education
The "Mightier Work" of Reconstruction   113

Epilogue
Back to the Library   145

ACKNOWLEDGMENTS   157

NOTES   163

INDEX   185

"Gruesome, Truthful, Yet Digestible"

EDUCATORS KNOW THAT EMOTIONS ARE part of the learning process. Teaching and learning Black history is emotional. Given the long history of degrading portrayals of Black people in US classrooms, and the powerful role that negative stereotypes of Black people continue to play in our society, many teachers are understandably interested in approaches to Black history that do not retraumatize, shame, or degrade Black students. Instead, they seek to make sure Black students learn about the past in ways that are joyful and show their ancestors as powerful and heroic.[1]

I wish that had been my experience. As a Black student in multiracial (but mostly white) elementary school classrooms, with mostly white teachers, I recall cringing whenever Black history came up as a topic. It is embarrassing to admit, but as a young person I was ashamed of my ancestors, who were, as far as I could tell, always on the bottom rung of life's ladder, always conquered, always defeated. The less they came up in the curriculum, as far as I was concerned, the better. If asked, I would let people know that I hated history. That didn't change until a classmate handed me a tattered copy of *The Autobiography of Malcolm X* in the hallways of my high school (saying, earnestly, "You need to read this"). I was hooked. The more I discovered about the brilliance of the United States' trenchant Black critics, starting with Malcolm, the more I felt inspired to keep learning.

My newfound pride in Black history has become tempered, over time, with the knowledge that Black people, like all people, have a messy, complicated past, full of heroism as well as compromise. Today, my emotional reaction to learning Black history runs along a wider spectrum, sometimes proud, sometimes horrified, and often saddened. Where before I saw only defeats, I now see a contest, an ongoing struggle, with highs and lows, and including some precious victories.

The ideas I present in this book are an attempt to process what I've learned, mostly as an adult, reading Black history while teaching it at many levels, from second grade through graduate school. I grappled with these topics alongside young people as a teacher of elementary grades in public schools in Harlem and Brooklyn. As a teaching artist, I helped high school students encounter, digest, and perform excerpts from primary documents collected in the anthology *Voices of a People's History of the United States*. When I began working full time as a researcher of Black education history, I shared my findings with undergraduate and graduate students in various

City University of New York courses that I taught. I learned even more about the long struggle to develop and defend Black studies programs in colleges and high schools, encountering new archival sources and the work of cutting-edge scholars while serving as associate director of education at the world-renowned Schomburg Center for Research in Black Culture. In several public history projects, and in my role as director of the Center for Educators and Schools at the New York Public Library, Black history remained the foundation of my work.

Many years before any of that work began, though, my interest in Black history was kindled in activist spaces, where the stakes of learning were very different. Long before I ever stepped into a classroom as a teacher, I took my seat, as a student, in coffee shops and church basements, reading and discussing books on Black history. With my meager wages, I began building a personal Black history library. I was trying to understand the past in a new way. I wasn't reading and writing to get a good grade or complete an assignment. I was working on my own assignment: to change the world. It was my commitment to making social change in the present that fueled my reading about the past. If I could figure out how oppression was made, I hoped to glean some knowledge about how to unmake it. If I could peer back in time at the ways that oppressed people fought back and won, I hoped to learn something about how I might contribute to doing the same. It took a long time for me to realize that history doesn't give us every answer we're looking for. It doesn't present us with ready-made solutions to today's thorny problems. The process of learning about the past is full of surprises, and even with the best of intentions, it is a humbling endeavor.

I was honored to have a seat at the table in the Schomburg Center's Scholars-in-Residence Program, researching and writing about the student movement at Tuskegee University, an explosive and radical history that unfolded in one of the nation's most important HBCUs (historically Black college or university). And I was incredibly fortunate to have the opportunity to join the staff at the Schomburg Center the following year. I didn't go to an HBCU, but spending four years at the Schomburg Center, a profoundly Black space (in many senses), was a transformative learning experience. I learned how joyful, intellectually challenging, and inspiring it is to be immersed in a center of Black-led creativity and scholarship. In addition to the brilliant staff members, working at the Schomburg Center exposed me daily to top scholars, new ideas, and a near-constant temptation to buy more books. The more I learned, the more I realized how little I knew. Ultimately, I came to believe that Black history is for everyone, because Black history is an invitation to rethink everything. But learning to see the world differently, learning to rethink what you think you know, isn't easy, and it doesn't always feel good.

Today, there are people who are making it even harder to learn. They advocate banning Black history, citing their perception that this teaching (or rather, the often-caricatured version of it) leads white students to "feel discomfort, guilt, or anguish or any other form of psychological distress on account of his or her race," as one recent piece of legislation framed the issue.[2] To this I think we must respond in two different ways. First, we must acknowledge that because our society and its classrooms have been so deeply invested in white supremacist mythology, central to which is the history of the United States, truly grappling with Black history will evoke strong feelings in students who are steeped in those myths. If you are a person whose sense of goodness is bound up with a belief in the righteousness of the United States and the unfailing heroism and genius of the white male political leaders who founded it, then, yes, learning to see this nation, its history, and its leaders in a new way is going to be jarring and perhaps upsetting. At the same time, as historian Robin D. G. Kelley notes, legislation aimed at protecting students from the "discomfort" that may result from studying Black history "never considers the psychological distress Black, brown, and Indigenous students frequently endure as a result of whitewashed curricula, tracking, suspensions and expulsions on the slightest pretext, even abuses by law enforcement inside their own classrooms."[3]

But, as I argue in this book, learning more about Black history is not about demonstrating that Black people are good and white people are bad. It does reveal that there were (and are) people who committed (and commit) atrocities, using racial ideology to rationalize them. It may seem counterintuitive, but one of the most interesting things to me about delving into Black history is that the deeper you go, the less credence you will give the idea that race is inherently meaningful. Teaching Black history, then, is not about training students to see themselves as members of essentialist racial categories. Rather, teaching Black history helps them to explore how these categories get created and re-created over time. We can think and talk and learn about these categories without believing in them.

The second response to those who would ban Black history builds on a useful analogy that the author Isabel Wilkerson often deploys, of thinking of us collectively as homeowners and the nation as our house.[4] If you buy a house with a rotten foundation, it may be upsetting to learn about it, but isn't it better to know? You may have felt better about your house when you were ignorant about the problems with its foundation. But doesn't that knowledge empower you to do something about it? What if the foundation collapses? Isn't it more likely that you'll feel better (and actually be safer) in the long run for having confronted the truth rather than remaining blissfully ignorant of it? Looking at it that way, it's clear that what underlies so much criticism of Black history is that people don't want to confront what social or political changes might be implied by looking more closely at the country's foundation. They don't want to have to do anything to fix the house.

Some may fear the study of Black history because they think that it undermines pride in the United States as a nation. Others may embrace Black history for opposite reasons—the hope that by studying the flaws in its foundation, the nation might be strengthened. Both of these agendas turn on the question of which is more patriotic—to defend the national myths or to confront them. This book goes further, however, to argue that patriotism is too narrow an ambition for Black history. Rather, its study shows us that the idea of a nation is as unstable as the category of race. The study of Black history, I believe, requires us to remain skeptical about the prospects of achieving our highest collective aspirations for freedom and democracy within the borders of the United States, or indeed of any nation.

In this country, there is a strong temptation to defend the study of Black history by pointing to the enduring loyalty of so many Black leaders and organizations to the United States. It is true that more often than not, Black people have framed their struggles as attempts to realize the promise of the stated ideals of the nation. That perspective remains the dominant paradigm in Black politics in the United States. In a 2016 Black history month address, then–US President Barack Obama expressed this idea, stating that Black history is about the ways that African Americans' lived experiences "have shaped and challenged and ultimately strengthened America."[5] At the same time, there were also many other important leaders and thinkers in Black history who challenged the relevance of patriotism. Activists like Malcolm X and Audley Moore looked to newly liberated African nations for political leadership, traveled to them, and tried to build internationalist, rather than nationalist, political agendas. Students of history can, will, and should draw their own conclusions; my point is that what educators consider acceptable lines of inquiry in Black history should not require loyalty to any nation as a thematic starting point.

There is a broad spectrum of patriotic Black history available to readers. Conservatives are fond of selectively quoting from Dr. Martin Luther King Jr. to build a case against affirmative action ("content of their character") and have, in my opinion, wrongly tried to paint the civil rights movement as a fundamentally anti-regulation, libertarian affair.[6] True, there are strains of free-market ideology in Black political thought, from Booker T. Washington to Geoffrey Canada and even Barack Obama (which have come to the fore recently in the field of education).[7] But the broader thrust of Black politics in this country, from the American Revolution to the present, has been to define "freedom" in terms of expanded democracy and guaranteed access to the means of life: land, wages, school, and health care. And although Black people's struggles for those things have helped many non-Black people get them, too, white people have largely been trained to view the matter, unfortunately, as a zero-sum game: Black people's gains, they too often believe, must mean losses for them.[8]

While trying to think outside of the national frame, this book mainly explores the history of the United States, which has been the focus of my reading and study and teaching. One exception is the Haitian Revolution. Whereas the American Revolution was led by slaveholders (in a British colony), the Haitian Revolution was made by people who were enslaved (in a French colony). They were, in the majority, people who were born in Africa and remembered their homelands; they did not internalize "slave" as an identity and, apart from the upper layers of leadership, did not care much about France. They left behind a written record substantially smaller than North American slaveholding revolutionaries like Thomas Jefferson, but their actions represented a greater break with the pattern of the modern world, and they are, arguably, the authors of our twenty-first-century conceptions of universal human rights and individual liberty. From their perspective, the 1776 revolution was not nearly as heroic. Critics may howl that this sort of discussion teaches young people to "hate America," without realizing that the stakes here have nothing to do with "hating" or "loving" the United States, or trying to prove that one nation is "bad" or another is "good." That this comes so quickly to our lips reveals how caught up we are in notions of national superiority, a cousin of the obsession with racial superiority. If we let go of superiority, and embrace humility, we become open to genuinely learning from others.

And letting go of superiority helps us learn about ourselves. It is comforting (to some people) to believe that the overthrow of slavery and later, of southern segregated schools, proves our national greatness, proves that we are only moving forward to greater freedom and justice, and never backward. But Black history, told from Black people's perspectives, forces us to revise these stories. In our classrooms, Reconstruction in the US South is another often-overlooked revolution.[9] When our historical narratives skip from slavery to Jim Crow, we miss a moment, several decades long, in which Black people and their allies turned the US South upside down. High on the priorities list of the newly liberated people was education, which they insisted should be free, tax supported, and available to everyone regardless of race. In many ways, we are still struggling to achieve the promise of multiracial democracy and of public education that Black people and their allies fought for in this period. It required tremendous violence to squash those dreams and to thwart the progress of Reconstruction. When white supremacist vigilantes like the Ku Klux Klan carried out widespread campaigns of political terrorism, among their targets were schools and teachers.

The counterrevolution succeeded and was a major setback for US democracy, but Black people consolidated some gains, particularly in the field of education, and against all odds continued building on their long-standing belief that education is a means of political liberation. The common misperception of the 1954 *Brown v. Board of Education* Supreme Court decision as the high-water mark for racial justice in education misses all of that. The process of desegregation that took place in the US South (not in the North, which successfully segregated schools by other means) was controlled by white elites, who viewed Black educators, leaders, parents, and students as inherently inferior. We do our students a disservice if we teach them that the idea of integrated schooling first appeared in 1954. In truth, we saw the promise of a democratic society and democratic education eighty years prior in a revolutionary moment when newly liberated Black people took the initiative, in an all-too-fleeting alliance with abolitionists in the Republican Party, to reconstruct the US South.

Most of us were raised on a curriculum shot through with white supremacy but never named as such. We were fed superiority-infused stories of race, of nation, stories of a heroic revolution in 1776, and of ever-expanding rights and freedoms. The simple shift of carrying on in class as though other people are fully human and equal can be a shock to the senses. But only supremacists experience steps toward equality as degradation. Black history is for everyone precisely because it is not about promoting a new kind of superiority. Instead, by seeing the past in a new way, Black history offers an opportunity to begin to see ourselves (whether you identify as Black or not) in a new way, too. What happens when we start to learn new stories? Who might we, then, become?

* * *

Anastacia, a Teen Reading Ambassador for the New York Public Library, asked: "Black history is often diluted or flat-out not taught in schools. . . . Do you think that the heavy truth should be taught in schools? And if so, what would be your advice to educators to be able to teach that truth to kids in a gruesome, truthful, yet digestible manner?"

I was sitting on my favorite stage in the world, in the Langston Hughes Auditorium of Harlem's Schomburg Center for Research in Black Culture, on a warm June morning. Across from me sat award-winning journalist and author Nikole Hannah-Jones. The auditorium was filled with roughly two hundred educators (and many more were watching the livestream). It was one of those days that New York City's public schools were closed so that teachers can have meetings and learn something new. My role was to ask Nikole questions during the opening event of a daylong program for educators, but Anastacia made my job easy. Nikole's response asserted the importance of teaching Black history, while recognizing the incompleteness of any historical narrative and the always-unfinished nature of learning about the past.

"OK, that was an excellent question," Nikole began. "Our youth will and do lead us." She continued, emphasizing that the "truths" we teach should be plural, not singular, given that "there could never be a single origin story of a place as diverse as the United States." Turning to the educators in the audience, she argued that the "primary obstacle to educators teaching this history well is not laws, it's lack of knowledge. It's folks who have not been educated on this area themselves very well, and so therefore cannot teach it with any level of sophistication."[10] In two recent national surveys, teachers essentially agreed: They are not as well prepared to teach Black history as they want to be.[11]

Learning history is not easy, especially when it challenges truths that we hold dear. Sometimes a more truthful history is gruesome, and educators often struggle to find ways to convey that truth while still making it digestible for others. But, as Nikole noted, the "truth" of the past is not fixed. Each story, each new perspective "is adding to our collective understanding and getting us closer to the truth," she said. "I think we should always be on the quest for truth, [while] knowing we'll never actually fully arrive there, because there's always more that we should know."

This book of essays is, in a sense, a record of my own quest for truth, an attempt to better understand myself, the United States, and the world. Have we always seen each other as distinct "races" of people? Can we truly live out the ideals of freedom and democracy within the borders of any nation? Are the Haitian Revolution and Reconstruction in the US South moments of hope or of horror? Or both? These are the questions I have been asking myself and trying to answer through reading, research, teaching, and learning.

* * *

In my journey as an adult learner of Black history, there came a moment when I realized that the authors whose books filled my shelves were mostly male. At the urging of (mostly women) colleagues, I began paying closer attention to the writings of women historians, and through my career I have had the privilege of meeting and dialoguing with some of them. Through this book I hope you, too, will encounter their names, ideas, and works. I see this book as a modest contribution to an expanding literature that, through investigating Black history, helps us to reexamine many other received categories of thought and being, including gender and sexuality. I could say the same for new works in Indigenous studies, disability studies, Latinx history, and other related fields, all of which add so much richness to our understanding of the world. I'm grateful to authors, thinkers, colleagues, and friends who are blazing these trails and sharing their work so that others, like me, may follow.

It's hard to overstate the importance of African history, particularly precolonial African history, in the teaching of Black history.[12] Africa and Africans play a large role in the stories that I'm telling in this book, as political thinkers and leaders in the context of the Haitian Revolution in the eighteenth and nine-teenth centuries, and in the twentieth-century struggles for independence and liberation on the continent. In both cases, as I discuss in this book, Black people in the United States looked to Africans for inspiration, ideas, and political leadership.

So, although I truly believe that Black history is for everyone, I recognize that my approach to sharing it has limitations, mainly due to the limitations of my own understanding at this moment in my journey as a learner. While I have endeavored to use my personal experiences as a guide in an effort to make the ideas more accessible, I also cite my sources throughout. They're an invitation to read more, to see for yourself, and to continue your own journey.

1

Race

Free People of Color

THE FIRST FRIEND I EVER had was a little boy named Matt. We were approximately four years old, and I vaguely remember that the walk from my house to his was not far. Matt interrupted our play one day with a suddenly serious look and tone that caught me by surprise. "Brian, you're brown," he declared unceremoniously, "and I'm peach." I certainly had no idea how to respond to this information, and to this day I marvel at his ability to summon "peach" to define himself. I related this story in a speech and, for laughs, imagined that my response was, "Well, these Legos aren't going to build themselves." In truth, I don't recall how I responded, or if I responded. And I don't remember that Matt had more to say on the matter. This little scene unfolded in Davenport, Iowa, where my family had relocated from Detroit, where I was born. In our new neighborhood, mine was one of the few families of color. Both of my parents are fair-skinned people who grew up in segregated, all-Black communities. Neither of my parents would have ever played with Matt's parents growing up. But I was raised in a different time and an entirely different social circumstance.[1]

Looking back on that strange playdate interlude, I imagine that Matt was probably trying to do me a favor. He was trying to introduce me to rules that are peculiar to children and well-known to grown-ups. If you didn't understand them, you'd find life in the United States very strange. You'd do things you shouldn't do, go places you shouldn't go. You'd mess up and embarrass yourself. The rules that govern the ideology of race in the United States are, of course, made up. They are inventions of human society, not of biology. For there to be a color line, someone must draw the color line. Someone must interrupt the play of children and impress upon them the importance of brownness, of peachness, and of knowing the difference.

* * *

The Naturalization Act of 1790 determined who got to call themselves an American citizen.[2] This act restricted citizenship to persons who had resided in the United States for two years, who could establish their good character in court, and who were white. This was not a matter of custom or culture, but of law. Here is some of the strange historical stitching that has brought us to our present moment. The statement of law that "any alien being a white person" was a candidate to enjoy the benefits of citizenship shows us both how an unequal society was made and how human categories of inequality were created and re-created. Even after the Civil War and the overthrow of slavery, courts ruled to explicitly uphold these categories.

The construction and reconstruction of racial categories is laid bare in countless court battles over racial identity. Many enslaved people saw a possible path to freedom through such legal battles. They brought "freedom suits" to court, claiming even just one free white ancestor, and, at times, winning their freedom on the basis of that lineage. Policing the boundary between Blackness and whiteness required constant vigilance, because in reality so many people were plausible members of either or both categories, and laying claim to whiteness meant freedom. But even the abolition of slavery did not destroy this legal paradigm. In the infamous *Plessy v. Ferguson* case of 1896, the US Supreme Court reaffirmed the legitimacy of having separate railroad cars for Black people and white people. Homer Plessy, who claimed both African and French ancestry (including refugees from the Haitian Revolution), purposefully seated himself in the whites-only section to test the law. While his action was designed to highlight the injustice of segregated public accommodations, the highest court in the land did not see it that way. Rather, they ruled that segregated seating was important for upholding the right of white people to be secure in the value of whiteness. The US Supreme Court believed that it was very important to be able to determine who was white and who was not. After all, the ability to be white was actually a form of property—whiteness, in other words, had real value, and its owners had an interest in retaining it. The court said in its decision that "if he be a white man, and be assigned to the color coach, he may have his action for damages from the company, for being deprived of his so-called property. If he be a colored man and be so assigned, he has been deprived of no property, since he is not lawfully entitled to the reputation of being a white man."[3] And this made sense to the all-white court, in 1896, because they understood the value of the reputation of being white.

But who is white? By the 1930s, so many different types of people had followed Plessy's example and sued for whiteness that the complexity of US law can only be described as absurd. An explanation of whiteness, excerpted from Corpus Juris (the "body of law") in 1934, reads:

> A White person has been held to include an Armenian born in Asiatic Turkey, a person of but one-sixteenth Indian blood, and a Syrian, but not to include Afghans, American Indians, Chinese, Filipinos, Hawaiians, Hindus, Japanese, Koreans, negroes; nor does white person include a person having one fourth of African blood, a person in whom Malay blood predominates, a person whose father was a German and whose mother was a Japanese, a person whose father was a white Canadian and whose mother was an Indian woman, or a person whose mother was a Chinese and whose father was the son of a Portuguese father and a Chinese mother.[4]

Yes indeed . . . white people!

As historian Barbara Fields once quipped in a seminar, "Race is real the same way Wednesday is real."

* * *

I grew up around a lot of white people. In elementary school, most of the Black students were in a general education "track" while I—and a handful of other Black students—was in a "gifted" class. I remember receiving the message, one way or another, that I was one of the acceptable ones; I was different. I remember the way this kind of backhanded compliment stung me, but it took me a long time to understand why it hurt. In truth, though, the comment rings true. I am "acceptable" by America's standards, or at least more so: my skin is light, most of the time I dress like a middle-class professional, and my manner of speech betrays a large degree of assimilation in the white American mainstream (for example, I use phrases like "manner of speech").

But as many others have learned, there is no amount of assimilation that can shield you from racism in this country. Throughout my life, something—the kink of my hair or my "attitude"—would mark me as inferior, worthy of ridicule, humiliation, or ostracism. I got in trouble a lot, and one teacher actually wrote on my report card that I was "amoral." In third grade, I had my first Black teacher, and she was a revelation. Ms. Brooks was a thoughtful, intellectual, justice-oriented teacher who may very well have set me on the path to writing this book. She did her own version of the infamous "eye color segregation" activity, in which students with different attributes were, temporarily, governed by different rules in the classroom. My classmates and I were outraged, naturally, and when we calmed down, she explained that it was a lesson in discrimination—one that I never forgot. As I recall, she also taught us to recite and interpret poetry from the Black Arts movement. Ms. Brooks even decided it was OK if I squirmed in my chair. My mother came to visit my class one day and was horrified to see my whole body perched on top of my little desk. Ms. Brooks told my mother that I was allowed to sit that way as long as I got my work done, and my mother relented. And perhaps because she, too, was a Black woman, I could tell that despite their different perspectives, my mom trusted her.

As I got older, I understood that my mother's vigilance had to do with her assumption of the omnipresence of racism. She was determined that I attend the very best schools and simultaneously assumed that I would be the object of discrimination there. She maintained an intense, vigilant determination to protect me from it. She monitored everything about my treatment in school, ready to leap into action at the slightest slight. Sometimes I thought she went too far. When I entered middle school, my mother let her disappointment be known that I had not, to that point in my education, been given a prominent speaking role in any school functions. So, thanks to my mother raising a fuss I had to give a speech to my entire middle school.

In high school I started wondering, as teenagers do, how people go about finding romantic partners. From what I could tell in movies and television shows—my principal sources of information—you had to be rich and white to be worthy of love. I was neither, so I was worried. Like many young Black people, I internalized the idea that I would have to be twice as good to get half as much respect. Much to my dismay, my Blackness seemed to be the salient thing about me. One of my classmates had a gift for inventing creative ways to make fun of my kinky hair, and he got enough people laughing to send me home in tears for a good part of my freshman and sophomore years of high school. I'm so grateful to good friends who saw me through this, and brilliant teachers who nurtured my curiosity. But racism still stalked the hallways and classrooms.

One year, one of the few Black students at my high school found a noose hanging in his locker. The culprit—a white student—was quickly discovered, and all he had to do to get out of trouble was issue a lame apology. I wasn't sure at the time what else should have been done, but I knew that what had happened didn't feel like justice. I convinced my best friend that we should wear black armbands in school to protest. This act didn't earn me greater respect, only greater ridicule. One of our teachers thought it was funny and even prompted our classmates, during class, to have a laugh at our expense: "Look at Jones," one teacher said, "starting a revolution."

I saw racism happening to others, but not to me. Looking back, I realize that, apart from my black armband episode, my survival strategy was to make myself as nonthreatening as possible. I became so well practiced in the art of not offending racist white people that I ceased to become outraged by them, at least when I was their target. I knew how to enter a store, to make eye contact with someone who worked there, to smile and say hello as if to say: "Don't worry, I'm not trying to steal anything." Somehow—I suppose from being followed in stores frequently—I learned not to carry books into a bookstore, not to walk through a store with bags that were not sealed or zippered shut, and so on.

Once, as a college student, I caught a flight back to school after a break, and two friends—both white women—agreed to pick me up at the airport. Upon arrival, I retrieved my duffel bag from baggage claim and started walking toward the exit when a man in plain clothes approached me. He flashed a badge and asked if he could look inside my bag. I was caught off guard and automatically reverted to my no-threat strategy: I consented.[5] He pulled me to the side, dropped to one knee, unzipped my bag and began ruffling through it, at which point I noticed that he was not alone—a mysteriously silent associate was standing nearby. This second man looked me up and down, as did some of my former fellow passengers. But soon enough the first man was zipping up my bag and returning it to me. "You fit the description of a drug smuggler we're looking for." I accepted this nonapology, pondered briefly the possibility that I really did have a more entrepreneurial doppelgänger, and left the airport.

I got into my friends' car and headed to campus. At some point, I think sooner rather than later, I let slip that something had happened in the airport. When I related the story, I was truly shocked at my friends' reaction: outrage and anger. They were, without hesitation, furious and indignant. "That is so fucked up," my friend spat. I nodded and agreed, and they continued. Privately, I wondered why I had reacted so differently, why I seemed to feel nothing. Was I so accustomed to being under greater surveillance and scrutiny that I had learned to accept the injustice of it? Years later when I read the question Black scholar W. E. B. Du Bois posed, "How does it feel to be a problem?"[6] I would answer secretly, for myself: numb.

* * *

There are not different biological races of people. The natural variations in features of human beings, skin color included, are real, of course, but do not coincide with "race" as we think of it. Skin color varies, but it was never a matter of systemic political importance until a few hundred years ago. The origins of humans and the origins of the idea of race are not the same story.

Human beings that look and smell the way we do evolved around two hundred thousand years ago in the African continent and began venturing to other parts of the globe around seventy-five to fifty thousand years ago. They settled in various parts of the earth and in bands of people that were, for the most part, cut off from each other. And as all travel was by foot, they mostly remained in the same places for thousands of years. By living in one spot, apart from other humans for many thousands of years, these groups actually did evolve to look differently from each other, for reasons that have to do with the various environments in which they found themselves.

There is no biological basis to the idea of "race," but there is a biological basis to the fact that people have different features. If you look at the world's people before the modern era of rapid transportation, before the era of people moving quickly all over the planet, of the land being carved up into political units that today we call "nations"—all of which are still very new in human history—there is a pattern: the people that settled near the equator, where they get the most intense direct sunlight, had darker complexions.

All human beings, regardless of their complexion (albinos excepted), have the ability to produce melanin as a protection from ultraviolet radiation. If you are fair skinned and subject to intense direct sunlight for prolonged periods, you are likely to develop skin cancer. Although there is a good chance skin cancer wouldn't become a problem until you're older, past your reproductive years, there is, however, evidence that ultraviolet radiation interrupts processes associated with folic acid (folate), which can cause birth defects and other problems. This suggests that darker complexions may have evolved to absorb ultraviolet radiation, and therefore protect not only from skin cancers but also from related interruptions to reproduction.[7]

On the other hand, if you're one of those people who has been living for thousands of years in regions far from the equator, regions of scarce or indirect sunlight, you have a different problem—the problem of vitamin D deficiency. The sun is a crucial source of vitamin D for humans, so you're going to have illnesses associated with vitamin D deficiency, such as heart conditions or weak bones. You actually need to absorb more sunlight, and so paler skin is advantageous in those places.

This is the only biological basis we can find between people who have different complexions around the world, but that's a far different thing from saying that people with different complexions actually comprise races of people in a biological sense. This is important because scientists have tried for a long time to prove that there are different biological races, and they have failed. Today, we even understand that there is more genetic diversity within the so-called races than between them. In their book *How Real Is Race?*, Carol C. Mukhopadhyay, Rosemary Henze, and Yolanda T. Moses write about how phenomena that we think of as demonstrating a biological basis of "race"—the idea that sickle cell anemia is a "Black" disease, for example—are just not true: "In the United States, the sickle cell gene is more common among African Americans than other populations—but it is not a 'racial' gene," they write. "The genetic variation that causes it is also found in parts of South Asia, southern Europe, and the Middle East. And it is found in only some areas in Africa." They also write about genetic diversity among what we call "Black" people:

> When we turn to the racial category "Black," we find enormous geographic and human variability—Africa has deserts, mountains, oceans, tropical areas, and spans a range of latitudes, some distant from the equator. It has hundreds, if not thousands, of linguistically, culturally, politically, and historically distinct populations. Africa is home to the shortest and the tallest people of the world. Other traits vary significantly, including skin color, facial traits (nose, eye shape), overall body shapes, even the frequency of sickle cell and lactose intolerance.[8]

Another problem with Americans' tendency to define who is what based on skin color is that skin color is not a discrete trait.

There's a spectrum, a gradation, of skin colors, and so marking off at an arbitrary point at which to say somebody paler than this belongs in one category and somebody darker is another is an act of arbitrarily creating a division among people. Nature, as the saying goes, abhors a category. The attempt to fit the square peg of race into the round hole of biology is why the logic of the 1934 Corpus Juris definition of a "white" person is so tortured.

Modern humans have been around for at least two hundred thousand years, but the idea of "race" as we know it today is a new development—only a few hundred years old. Some scholars argue that anti-Black racism is older, emphasizing the continuity between modern racism and older forms of prejudice. In my reading, the rupture between those older hatreds and the development of race as an ideology through the Atlantic trade in human beings from Africa, which I describe next, is more convincing. If two hundred thousand years of human history were a two-hundred-page book, the modern idea of "race" begins in the last paragraph on the last page. And while a full accounting must take into account the ways anti-Black racism took shape all over the Atlantic world, in many ways the story truly starts here, in North America.[9]

* * *

At the beginning of the 1620s, after nearly two decades of trying to get rich quick through mining, pillaging, and looking for gold, European settlers found a new way to accomplish the same thing: growing tobacco for export. The state of Virginia, the first "cell" of the organism that became the United States of America, began as a business venture. And, as Barbara Fields notes, one didn't get rich in Virginia growing tobacco by democratic means. The most profitable thing to do was to force people into the growing of it. "Whatever truths may have appeared self-evident in those days," Fields wrote, "neither an inalienable right to life and liberty nor the founding of government on the consent of the governed was among them."[10] First, Virginia colonists tried to press Indigenous people into this labor, but that failed—the Native people were on their home turf, they knew the land better, and they could escape. Native Americans were not a reliable source of the kind of intense labor power the Virginia colonists needed.

But what was behind the urgency to produce so much tobacco in the first place? The problem wasn't that the colonists were addicted to cigarettes; this was not about growing leaf to smoke. Rather, they were addicted to profits; this was about cultivating tobacco to sell. This was production for the world market, at the pace of the world market, for unseen tobacco consumers thousands of miles away. As they piled up unimaginable wealth wrenched from the sweat and blood of laborers, these colonists—and their peers in the Caribbean and later in the Mississippi Valley and other coastal regions—were bringing into existence a new normal: a world in which people used money to buy things made in distant places, using wages earned from making things for other people, connected only through the market. Buying what you don't make, and making

what you don't buy. In other words: alienated commodity production and consumption on a mass scale. Cotton for cloth-
ing, sugar to sweeten food and drink, and tobacco to smoke.
Elites had long enjoyed luxuries from distant lands, but now,
for the first time, millions more people would develop a taste
for new necessities of everyday life that were produced a world
away and could only be acquired by cash.[11]

The settlers also tried to coerce their fellow Englishmen
into performing this labor, through a category of unfree labor
known as indentured servitude. Sometimes they arranged for
poor Englishmen to be kidnapped and brought to the colony
for this purpose. Indentured servants were essentially property: they could be bought and sold, traded, they could be
offered as stakes in card games, they could be whipped or
even murdered by their masters. But this system, too, had
problems and limitations, mostly because indentured servitude was temporary and, if the servants survived (they didn't
always), they, too, could become landowners and therefore
competitors to their former masters. Why not enslave them?
"Because they were white" doesn't work as an explanation.
Pushing one's own countrymen down to the level of a slave
was not beyond the pale (the British Parliament debated
whether or not to enslave the poor), but would have provoked
controversy in England (where the decision would have to be
ratified) and would have ratcheted up the class struggle there
(soon to be engulfed in its own civil war) quite a bit. Among
the unfortunate consequences of such a contest would be the
potential loss of the labor supply.[12]

So the settlers, thirsty for a steady supply of labor to make their dreams of riches come true, finally hit upon the idea of bringing Africans to Virginia. For a long while these Africans came not from Africa directly but from the Caribbean, where the Portuguese had already done the dirty work of enslaving them. Historian Ira Berlin described these Africans as "Atlantic creoles"—often fluent in European languages and customs from experience working in a variety of Atlantic coastal regions.[13]

It may shock the reader to learn that some of these Africans became free and lived well in that seventeenth-century Virginia colony. The colonists purchased Africans to do the hard labor, but neither law nor custom nor ideology immediately dictated that Africans always and in every case be locked into a subordinate status for life. A small number of Africans became free. And, in the absence of systematic oppression, they did what others did—they worked to become successful members of the community. Anthony Johnson arrived in Virginia in 1621 as "Antonio a Negro" and was one of the lucky few to not only survive but win the favor of his master and earn enough on the side to buy his freedom. Thirty years later, in 1651 he was "Anthony Johnson," owner of 250 acres of land and at least one slave.[14] Landowning free men of African descent, like Johnson, could and did petition the courts when they needed to do so. Free Africans could and did bring lawsuits against Europeans—then called "Christians"—and win. There are records of Africans adopting Christian babies (it's only later that language changed from "free" and "slave" or "African" and "Christian" to "white" and "Black"). In the fierce competition for land and labor it was not easy to rise from the status of servant or even slave to that of planter, but it was legally possible. But by the end of the seventeenth century, as mortality rates declined and life expectancy rose, indentured servants from Europe became scarcer, making the purchase of people kidnapped from Africa at a higher price a better bargain, and the logic of the situation changed.[15]

Once the cost structure shifted, people kidnapped from Africa became the primary source of agricultural labor in the colony. Instead of attempting to further wring every possible drop of labor from their fellow colonists, the planters could now enlist them in the joint enterprises of stealing land and labor. They rewarded their fellow colonists for fighting the Indigenous people and taking more land for agriculture. They hired colonists to manage and carry out the importation of people from Africa as the near-exclusive labor force to work the newly acquired land. And so, slowly, a new way of life developed, as did new ideas to rationalize it. For the first time in human history, the color of one's skin was given a systematic political significance. Anti-Black prejudice was not new in European history, but it was never systematic or institutionalized, because there was no social structure or way of life that required systemic anti-Black prejudice. Now, at the end of the seventeenth century in colonial Virginia, there was a very good reason (from the master's point of view) to assign a political significance to dark skin—it was an ingenious way to brand someone as a slave. It is a brand that the enslaved person could never wash off, erase, or run away from. There

was no way out. The capitalist, commodity-producing plantation needed unfree labor and, through trial and error, settled
on unfree African labor.

Even so, it is important to recognize that this was a process
that took time. When I'm teaching this history, I often share
a timeline of slave laws in early colonial Virginia. You don't
bother to write down a law to stop people from doing something they never do or can't do. Like a child constantly changing the rules of a game when he isn't winning, the Virginia
Slave Code shows us, by its prohibitions, the existing behavior
that was widespread enough to be a problem. A 1660 law stipulated that English servants who ran away with "negroes" would
have to make up the lost labor time for the masters of both. In
1662, the law was updated to double the times of service for the
same offense. And while they were busy passing laws to punish voluntary unions between English and Africans, planters
were sure to legislate their right to rape. In 1662, the legal code
specified that the status of children would follow the condition
of the mother. Thus, any offspring resulting from the rape of
women held as property would only increase the property of
the planter.[16] In these ways, the leaders of the Virginia colony
institutionalized anti-Black racism because it was useful and
profitable. But there was another reason to draw a color line
throughout their society: they were afraid.

"Bacon's Rebellion" should be taught alongside the American Revolution and the Civil War as a crucial turning point
in this country's history. Both the rebellion and the aftermath
are revealing about the colony that seeded the new nation.

Virginia's well-armed young white propertyless men were a constant source of danger to the elites. In 1676, they rose up and nearly destroyed the colony. Interestingly, a number of Africans joined the rebellion. But this was no socialist revolution. It was a conflict between Virginia's governor, Sir William Berkeley, and a landowner, Nathaniel Bacon, who wanted a more aggressive policy toward the Indigenous people and the seizure of more of their lands than the governor thought expedient. Bacon appealed to the propertyless whites, rallied them to his cause, promised liberty and plunder to servants and enslaved people, and in short order his impromptu army outnumbered Berkeley's and the rebels proceeded to burn and sack Jamestown. Colonial Virginia was a tinderbox of grievances, and Nathaniel Bacon lit the fuse. When British troops finally arrived, they were able to quell the rebellion, but a band of twenty English servants and eighty enslaved people refused to submit. They were captured and returned to their owners.[17]

After suppressing the rebellion, the planters moved more decisively to put divisions into law and to categorize people to make it difficult, if not impossible, for them to see each other as allies, let alone rebel together. So they made a new rule: only white people were allowed to own property, own guns, participate in juries, and serve on militias. A law of 1680 stipulated that no "negroe" could own weapons or ever raise a hand to (i.e., strike, hit) any Christian, while negroes who ran away could now lawfully be killed. A 1691 law said that any negroe-Christian married couple had to leave the colony within three months of the marriage. According to a law passed in 1705, all non-Christian servants brought to the colony were considered "real estate" and could be lawfully killed by their masters. Year upon year, the planters drew a legal line between what we know today as "white" and "Black" people. But what about the free negroes like Anthony Johnson?

Thanks to Nikole Hannah-Jones and *The New York Times*'s 1619 Project, more readers and students have become familiar with the fact that the very first "twenty and odd" Africans were brought to the Virginia colony in that year. We know that Anthony Johnson arrived just two years later. But how long would you guess Virginian colonists took to write down a law to explicitly prevent landowning Africans like Johnson from voting? The answer should give us pause. The year was 1723—more than one hundred years after that first ship full of captives reached Virginia's shores. If racism were more of an automatic, built-in part of the way humans relate to each other, we might expect the colonists to get to work setting up slavery as a condition for life for Africans sooner; allowing Africans to own land in the colony and be part of the voting public should have been unthinkable. Instead, the fact that disfranchisement of Africans in colonial Virginia was a century-long process shows us that the kind of systemic, institutional racism that we know today was not automatic; it had to be built, brick by brick.

It may be even more surprising to learn that the actions of the Virginia legislature, for some white people, at least, violated common sense. For at least some of them, racialized slavery, and the laws set up to reinforce it, were not so easily swallowed.

Listen to the words of the attorney general (not just any white man, but an elite, powerful white man) of Virginia, objecting to the 1723 law that disfranchised free, land-owning "negroes":

> I cannot see why one freeman should be used worse than another, merely upon account of his complexion . . . ; to vote at elections of officers, either for a county, or parish, &c. is incident to every freeman, who is possessed of a certain proportion of property, and, therefore, when several negroes have merited their freedom, and obtained it, and by their industry, have acquired that proportion of property, so that the above-mentioned incidental rights of liberty are actually vested in them, for my own part, I am persuaded, that it cannot be just, by a general law, without any allegation of crime, or other demerit whatsoever, to strip all free persons, of a black complexion (some of whom may, perhaps be of considerable substance,) from those rights, which are so justly valuable to every freeman.[18]

I don't know who this man had in mind when he referred to negroes "of considerable substance," but it tells us something about the effort required to create a system of white supremacy that a white man could rise to such a high station in colonial Virginia and conclude that it would not be "just" to strip someone of rights "without any allegation of crime" but merely according to their complexion. We are accustomed to thinking about this the other way around—that the ideas came before the action: Africans, we usually think, were enslaved and denied rights because of a preexisting prejudice, because they were different. But there is strong evidence that the causation was reversed: It was because kidnapping and enslaving Africans on a mass scale, year after year, was so profitable that racist ideas about Africans became necessary.

Until the plantation system took off in Virginia and Africans became enslaved for life, it was common for them to work alongside English indentured servants. As we have seen, the legislature repeatedly worked overtime to stop them from running away together. Like coworkers everywhere, they shared more than work. The voluntary intimacy of enslaved people and servant was the largest source of children of mixed descent in these years—not rape by masters.[19] No wonder Nathaniel Bacon considered calling upon them to fight together a plausible strategy in building his rebellion. It is not difference itself that creates systemic prejudice and double standards. It is not race that creates racism. Rather it is racism that creates race. The impulse to oppress and exploit is the wellspring from which the ideas about the oppressed and exploited take hold.

Over the years, as Virginia became a society based on racialized slavery, the space for Anthony Johnson's descendants and other free families of African descent to live in peace diminished, and they fled to Maryland and North Carolina.[20] Among those free families of color who left the nation's first colony were some of my ancestors.

* * *

Genealogy holds a special meaning for African Americans. The act of reconstructing our family trees always seems to hit up against a wall: slavery. Our ancestors, held as property, were documented as such. Enslaved people were commodities—they could be, and were, bought and sold. A master might keep spouses with each other or parents with their children, or they might not, depending on how badly they needed the money a sale might bring. After the Civil War, many accounts report freedpeople walking (in some cases, hundreds of) miles in search of family. Connecting what had been broken—family—was a top priority. Family, kinship, and social links were broken on both sides of the Atlantic. Slaveholders' need to dehumanize their human property meant attempting to erase the African past. American and European leaders followed suit: their scientists, their intellectuals, their historians, dismissed Africa, and held up Europe as the font of wisdom, industry, and genius. Thus, for Black people in the twenty-first century, researching our roots, reclaiming ancestors, making connections with cousins, however distant, can feel like an act of resistance, a small way of reasserting our humanity. The geometry of genealogy, however, is daunting for anyone. Biologically speaking, we all have a mother and a father, four grandparents, eight great-grandparents, sixteen great-great-grandparents, thirty-two great-great-great grandparents, and so on. Drawing a family tree gets very complicated very quickly, requires pruning to be intelligible, and becomes as much a product of subtraction as addition.

Contemporary research tools and websites built for this purpose make the work easier nowadays, but there is still a lot of guesswork involved in following the story of a person's life across documents that spell their name different ways, with the same name but different birth dates, and so on.[21] And then there is the emotional process. There is shame, embarrassment, and sadness, seeing the census indicate that an ancestor was a white man and a slave owner. There is the way one's breath catches when evidence emerges that a relative was enslaved. And, although I do not subscribe to national chauvinism, I admit that I took pleasure in discovering that, unlike most of the people I know, all sixteen of my great-great-grandparents were born in the United States, and all in just three states: North Carolina, Kentucky, and Tennessee. I see evidence that nineteen out of thirty-two of my great-great-great-grandparents were born in those same states, and I think it is likely that the rest were as well. I am, deeply, a product of this country. I think all people anywhere in the world have the right to criticize the United States (especially given the lethality of its heavy hand abroad), and I don't have time for "love it or leave it" or "outside agitator" paradigms, but I can't help but look at those thirty-two names and feel a twinge of righteous indignation. The oldest birth year I have found, among that generation, is 1775. More than two and a half centuries in this land is enough time to say that we, collectively, deserve better.

I tried to reach back further, but with each step backward in time the documentary record became thinner. Of the sixty-four ancestors (great-great-great-great-grandparents) to whom I directly owe my existence, I have only been able to find some archival records for sixteen. What I can glean about the life stories of those sixteen captivated me. They include white people who enslaved people, white people who did not, Black people who were enslaved, free Black people, and others whom I suspect were Indigenous. Of those sixteen, four were born in Virginia: two before the Revolutionary War, when Virginia was still a British colony (1756 and 1764) and two after (1777 and 1803). One of those men, James Nickens, was a free man of color in Virginia who fought in the war that made the new nation. But by the end of the century, he and his wife, Mary Peggy (who was also born in Virginia) must have decided that the growing regime of racialized slavery foreclosed any possibility for a future in the land of their birth. James and Mary choose to leave. Their son, my great-great-great-grandfather, Henry William Nickens, was born in Hertford, North Carolina, in 1799.

People of African descent—formerly enslaved people liberated in the course of English–Spanish colonial conflicts—settled in the area since the late 1500s, where they mingled with Indigenous Chowanoke people; as Virginia colonists conquered more and more of their land, Meherrin people fled in the early 1700s and settled in Hertford as well.[22] All four of my paternal great-grandparents were born there, and I know for sure that six of their parents were, too. Slavery was legal in North Carolina, but the law also continued to recognize free people of color.

Hertford might have seemed like an oasis of freedom at the dawn of the nineteenth century. A legislative act to take away the vote from free men of color, like the one Virginia passed in 1723, did not appear in North Carolina until 1835 (North

Carolina was the last state to pass such a law). "Free people of color" was defined broadly. It included Indigenous people, people of East Indian descent, people of African descent, and the families and children resulting from their unions. Crucially, free men of color in North Carolina could also own property. In a nation governed by the logic of white supremacy and racialized slavery, there was little social, political, or economic space for free people of color. In North Carolina, there was just a bit more. And so they came. According to the 1790 census there were just 216 free people of color in Hertford County, and seventy years later, on the eve of the Civil War, Hertford was one of seven counties in North Carolina with more than one thousand people counted that way.[23]

I write that people were "counted that way" because I know very little about how people identified themselves. The census and other records tell us how authorities categorized people, and it's worth pausing to acknowledge that this is an important part of the way the idea of "race" works—it is imposed. Jasper Wyatt and Catherine Ballah share a birth year: 1768. Jasper was recorded by the 1820 census as a "free white male" born in Delaware, and Catherine was born in Wales. They met as teenagers somewhere in North Carolina and started a family. Their daughter Anna was born in Hertford in 1783 and was almost certainly what we would call a "white" person. But Anna settled down with William Weaver, a man from a large family of people "of color" who also had also fled Virginia. According to some sources, the Weaver family begins with three brothers from the East Indies who emigrated to colonial Virginia in the late seventeenth century. Over time, through intermarriage with Indigenous people and people of African descent, they became "of color." By 1820, William and Anna had a daughter, Mary Weaver. The 1830 census did not record any white people or enslaved people in William's household, but did indicate nine unnamed free people of color, presumably including his wife, Anna, who had previously been recorded as "white." William died in 1840, so the 1850 census listed Anna as the head of household. Now, she and the two children still living with her were all identified the same way: "mulatto." When Anna Wyatt, my great-great-great-grandmother, became Anna Weaver, she passed out of whiteness.

What she passed into, however, was not exactly Blackness. Living as exceptions to the rule of racialized slavery, free people of color in North Carolina faced ostracism, legal censure, and violence from radical proslavery white people. They kept to themselves, creating a world of their own in the margins of the white world and in the shadow of slavery. Fair complexions became a mark of their distinct status. Their phenotypical proximity to whiteness set them apart from darker, unfree counterparts and even set them apart from each other. The pattern of colorism endured, even after the Civil War. My paternal grandmother and grandfather were both born in Hertford County, about eight miles apart (in 1906 and 1903, respectively). "As it turns out, more than distance separated Ruth and Aaron," my father wrote of his parents. "Aaron and members of his family being of a darker complexion attended

Philippi Baptist Church while Ruth's family with the lighter skin attended Pleasant Plains Baptist Church."[24] "Passing" for white became an endeavor fraught with risk but with great potential rewards. Ruth's brother passed for white, married a white woman, and to keep his secret would only visit his mother at night.

All identities are part imposition, part negotiation. We are all carefully coached from an early age in dress, behaviors, and language appropriate to an assigned identity (gender, race, nationality, class). The imposition is often made by church, law, or school, and enforcement becomes normalized all the way down to daily intimate interactions with community and family. But once a category is imposed, the negotiating begins. Some react to the imposition by rejecting the category for their own self-identification (Dominican or African immigrants bristling at being associated with Black Americans, for example). Others embrace identification with a category but challenge its subordination ("We're here, we're queer!" or "Black Power!").[25] As Barbara and Karen Fields observe, thinking about the politics of race purely as a matter of identity is insufficient because its imposition from others often trumps self-identification.[26] If Homer Plessy thought of himself as a white man, that wouldn't change how he was treated on the train.

Sometimes the imbalance between racial self-identification and racial imposition, between how people see you and how you see yourself, is perilous. The celebrated author Edwidge Danticat emigrated to the United States from Haiti as a child, and personally knew Abner Louima, who was arrested, beaten, and sexually assaulted by Brooklyn police officers in 1997. The Black immigrant parents she knew "harbored the illusion that if their émigré and US-born children are the politest, the best dressed, and the hardest working in school, they might somehow escape incidents like this."[27]

Not all self-identifications are created equal. Pride in Blackness, for Black people, is often an essential starting point for challenging racism and inequality. Yes, it can lead some toward essentialist ideas, including a belief in the biological basis of race. But the thrust of Black pride, like Black Power and Black Lives Matter, is to challenge the structures of racism and white supremacy. The very fact that the slogan "Black Lives Matter" must be spoken at all, and that it provokes such a reflexive, defensive response, is instructive. I hope that, by now, you don't need to be told that "White Lives Matter" or "White Power" or "White Pride" are slogans without any redeeming value. They are claims to an identity that is bound up with slave ownership, with being on top, with dominating, oppressing, and exploiting. "All Lives Matter" also lacks redeeming value as a slogan. It is not actually a call to make all lives matter. We know this because the voices shouting "all lives matter" use it as a counterclaim, hurled from the sidelines of marches against racism, never from within them. We will truly know that all lives can matter when non-Black people can pronounce the phrase "Black Lives Matter" and take concrete action—and real risks—to make it so.

* * *

We often speak about this as a problem that has to do with race, or intolerance, or ignorance. It does not. Instead, it has to do with the housing market, and the school system, and health care, and jobs, and the way we rationalize the fact that our lives are organized as a competitive scramble. It is the fatal coupling, as geographer and activist Ruth Wilson Gilmore puts it, of power and difference.[28] Of course, all other things being equal, it is better to have a society where people can grow up around and get to know folks who are different from them in various ways, and in the process learn to appreciate our differences as well as our commonalities. But even ignorant grown-ups can learn to get along with each other if we give them half a chance. The problem is that we don't.

Our society must have poverty and crime and vulnerability and insecurity because our economic life is organized as a competitive scramble, and instead of indicting the scramble, we assign the meaning of success or failure to individuals—or, for even more stability, to groups of individuals. If we don't inscribe those meanings into someone's skin, the whole game might come crashing down. Blackness means crime, bad neighborhoods, bad attitudes, bad schools, low test scores, poverty, bad health, and bad habits. People learn that avoiding those things requires avoiding Black people. They also learn that fixing those things requires fixing Black people. But Black people are not the problem. Black people are just people, as prone to genius or to folly as anyone. Yet, by systematically structuring life's competitions so that Black people come out on bottom, the cause and effect seem to be reversed, and the architects of the game are let off the hook. Instead of happening to Black people, the bad things seem to emanate from Black people themselves, as if dark skin was a magnet, attracting subprime loans, crumbling school buildings, and bullets. As if Blackness were a kind of powerful, unshakable curse, following its wearers wherever they fled.

They fled Virginia for North Carolina. They fled North Carolina in search of jobs in Detroit, Michigan. Perhaps when my not-too-dark Black family moved from Detroit into Matt's nearly all-white Iowa town, some of the neighbors worried that the curse of Blackness would rub off on their property values or their kids' test scores. Perhaps Matt overheard the grown-ups talking and decided to share his distillation of the essential bit: "You're brown and I'm peach." Little Matt of course had no idea that peach people had been labeling my people for centuries. He couldn't have yet known that those labels were backed up by the force of law. The labels were his to impose and mine to negotiate, and I have been doing so ever since, and certainly will until I perish.

Black history is not about being stuck in these categories, but about seeing our way through them more clearly. History helps us see that the problem is not race, but racism. The problem is that white supremacy is not just a bad idea, it is a way of life. This way of life has proved to be both remarkably resilient and highly combustible. Each time the tinderbox that is this nation explodes, we have an opportunity to change that way of life.

2

Nation

"Your National Greatness"

IN THE SUMMER OF 1852, six hundred mostly white people
gathered in Corinthian Hall, Rochester, New York's premiere
lecture arena. The speaker they came to hear was Frederick
Douglass, who liberated himself from enslavement fourteen
years earlier, taught himself to read and write, started a newspaper, and became one of the nation's most well-known and
influential persons. The date was the fifth of July, but the occasion was the Fourth of July, the nation's birthday. "He who
could address this audience without a quailing sensation,"
Douglass began, with false modesty, "has stronger nerves than
I have."[1] Douglass continued to deliver a thirty-two-page solil-
oquy, which, as planned, he later republished in his newspaper
and also sold separately as a pamphlet. His conclusion was a
scathing indictment, seething with outrage at a nation that celebrated its founding as a righteous blow against tyranny and
oppression while simultaneously holding millions of people in

chains. "What, to the American slave, is your 4th of July?" Douglass asked. "I answer," he continued,

> a day that reveals to him, more than all other days in the year, the gross injustice and cruelty to which he is the constant victim. To him, your celebration is a sham; your boasted liberty, an unholy license; your national greatness, swelling vanity; your sounds of rejoicing are empty and heartless; your denunciations of tyrants, brass fronted impudence; your shouts of liberty and equality, hollow mockery; your prayers and hymns, your sermons and thanksgivings, with all your religious parade, and solemnity, are, to him, mere bombast, fraud, deception, impiety, and hypocrisy—a thin veil to cover up crimes which would disgrace a nation of savages. There is not a nation on the earth guilty of practices, more shocking and bloody, than are the people of these United States, at this very hour.[2]

More than 150 years later, Douglass's words continue to circulate, but in a way he could not have imagined: reenactments of the speech in classrooms and in front of live audiences, and even more unpredictable from the nineteenth-century vantage, short clips from video recordings of those reenactments actually reach a global audience through social media. I have frequently had the honor of being one such reenactor, reciting a short excerpt of this speech before public audiences large and small. I do so under the auspices of an organization, Voices of a People's History of the United States, which sponsors public performances of powerful primary texts created by activists, dissenters, and rebels throughout US history.[3] My excerpted version ends with the damning words, "for revolting barbarity and shameless hypocrisy, America reigns without rival."[4] One of my first public performances of this speech was in the fall of 2004.[5] The disastrous US invasion and occupation of Iraq was just one year old, the war in Afghanistan was only in its third year, and the revolting barbarity of these wars was already as evident as the shameless hypocrisy of the so-called "War on Terror."

In 1852, Douglass certainly feigned apprehension as he rose to the podium, but for me the quailing sensation was real. The Concert Hall at the New York Society for Ethical Culture holds about eight hundred people, and on that late October day, it was packed. Reading the introductory text for my piece was none other than the revolutionary historian Howard Zinn, and I sat on stage with an incredible cast that included actor Leslie Silva, actor and writer Wallace Shawn, and Paul Robeson Jr., son of the legendary singer, actor, and activist. I was nervous, but eager to carry my weight in the company. To steady myself, I thought of Douglass's incredible journey of self-emancipation from enslavement, and then my thoughts leapt forward to the present. Long after the abolition of slavery, the speech continues to resonate with the persistent pattern of whitewashed national wrongdoing. I have frequently encountered social media posts remixing Douglass's rhetorical query to the tune of a new outrage perpetrated in the name of the nation: "What to the [insert: refugee denied asylum or child separated from parents at the border or unarmed Black person gunned down by police] is the fourth of July?" When I, as Douglass, thundered from the lectern that the Fourth of July celebrations amounted to "a thin veil to cover up crimes which would disgrace a nation of savages," I suspect I wasn't the only one in the concert hall thinking of the savagery of the mounting death toll in the Middle East, carried out in the name of the nation.

* * *

The enemies of Black history like to claim that it is "anti-American," but is it? Black history's censors might, for example, disagree that this Douglass speech has contemporary resonance, preferring to emphasize the fact that slavery was, eventually, overthrown—thereby demonstrating the nation's ability to right its own wrongs. Some of Black history's defenders shoot back: no, Black history is American history. That seems unassailable, and a useful step forward given the legacy of whitewashing US history. But is Black history necessarily "American"?[6] Does the study of Black history tend to be "pro-" or "anti-" the United States in some meaningful sense? What does Black history have to teach us about the relationship of Black people to the United States?

The "national greatness" of the United States, to the extent one can argue in support of it, lies principally in the ideals for which it is supposed to stand: democracy, personal liberty, and equality before the law. And yet, it should be common knowledge that the United States has actively prevented democracy, has actively denied personal liberty, and has systematically and explicitly refused to guarantee equality before the law, particularly (although not exclusively) for Black people within its borders. There is ample cause for Black people to describe themselves, as they often have, as "a nation within a nation." But, remarkably, that hasn't made Black people, overall, disloyal to the nation. Rather, Black people remain a "nation" that is, arguably, more loyal to the ideals of the larger nation than that larger nation itself.

Who supported and worked for the complete abolition of slavery and the federal guarantee of personal liberty more consistently than those whose personal liberty was nonexistent because of enslavement? What are the concepts of birthright citizenship and universal equality before the law, if not the fruits of Black people's striving through the Abolition movement, the US Civil War, and Radical Reconstruction?[7] Who pushed for and promoted the building of schools, hospitals, and other public institutions available to all, for the first time in the US South?[8] Who successfully championed new and stronger legislation securing equal access to public accommodations, stronger enforcement of civil rights and of voting rights? Who, furthermore, called for and campaigned for an Economic Bill of Rights for All Americans that would have guaranteed free access to higher education, free health care, and a guaranteed income to all?[9] And today, whose personal and civil liberties are most consistently abrogated by police, prosecutors, and prisons? And who is therefore at the forefront of the movement to reform (and for some, to abolish) these institutions of unfreedom in the land of the free? Black people are, in each case, the answer. Black people have been the most consistent force in US history for democratizing this democracy.

Black people have often sought to carry out this agenda through the nation's organized embodiment: the state. They took advantage of the conflict between northern capitalists and southern slaveholders to put their freedom on the agenda. Refusing to work en masse, escaping to Union Army camps in overwhelming numbers, they forced the North into fighting a war of liberation that it had tried to avoid. One hundred years later, Black people brought the business of Jim Crow to a halt through collective action, and once again dragged reluctant federal forces into intervening on their behalf in the South. Jim Crow segregation was broken as much by the moral example of nonviolent civil disobedience as by the federal troops who finally showed up with rifles and bayonets to enforce the law. If "states' rights" has been code for the "freedom" to oppress, discriminate, and exploit, "federal oversight" has been code for "intervention by the nation on behalf of Black people."

And despite the tendency of the US state to be systematically violent toward Black people, it is simultaneously the institution (or, the collection of institutions) that has provided the greatest opportunities for Black people. In the federal government and its agencies, they have found shelter, materially and symbolically, from the kind of racist violence and hyperexploitation that have long characterized North American capitalism. Whether you look at the postal service, or the various branches of the armed forces, or education, public sector jobs, much more reliably than private sector ones, have provided Black people with opportunities for advancement.[10] As of this writing, the majority of Black women with professional employment work within the public sector.[11] As public servants, Black people have, quite literally, joined the state.

Black people's loyalty to the federal government might be less complicated were it not for the fact that the same institutions in which we are now so deeply embedded had not also investigated, surveilled, disrupted, murdered, and destroyed Black activists and Black organizations and movements. One example of this trend is the history of Black people's claims for reparations for slavery and the slave trade: every single organized attempt to campaign for reparations in this country has been actively repressed by the US federal government.[12] Even Black historical figures who today are hallowed national heroes were, in their own time, targeted by the federal government. The Reverend Dr. Martin Luther King Jr., the only individual honored with both a federal holiday and a statue on the National Mall, was, while he was actually alive, the subject of intense surveillance by the Federal Bureau of Investigation, which tried to convince him to commit suicide.[13] And despite the moral high ground captured by the Black Lives Matter movement—a phrase uttered, for a time, by major corporations and displayed on suburban lawn signs—the activists who filled the nation's streets and kept those three words on the nation's lips are once again targeted by the national police, which claims to be protecting us from "Black identity extremists."[14]

Again and again, Black people's loyalty to the nation has been unrequited, particularly when national "unity" is at stake. Perhaps the most egregious example of national unity forged at our expense is the manner in which white men in both northern and southern states, trying to find a way forward in the aftermath of the Civil War, decided that white supremacy in the form of Jim Crow would be the glue binding together the very nation that Black people had just fought to save. "Just as the Negro gained his emancipation and new rights through a falling out between white men," historian C. Vann Woodward observed in 1955, "he now stood to lose his rights through the reconciliation of white men."[15] This pattern survives today in the commonsense notion that the reasonable "middle" of American politics, where we all counseled to meet, is a place where Black people's demands and slogans are disposable in the name of accommodating the influence of white supremacy.

* * *

Frederick Douglass simultaneously castigated the nation and believed in it. The first part is easy to understand, but what about the second? The laws and highest courts endorsed his enslavement, and the armed forces secured his bondage. He escaped, mastered the language of his oppressors, and used it against their system of slavery, telling his story back to the nation that had hunted him. Amazingly, although persecuted by the nation, Douglass did not believe it to be irredeemable. Douglass found, in the words of the Constitution, a logic of abolition. When the slave owners threatened to tear the country apart, Douglass was transformed from a fiery itinerant activist to a foremost spokesperson for the nation's second founding. During the war, Douglass was twice invited to the White House by the president. Contrary to the views of his former comrades who believed the country's legal foundation to be fundamentally proslavery, the Civil War seemed to vindicate Douglass's position. "Men talk of the Negro problem," Douglass opined. "There is no Negro problem. The problem is whether the American people have honesty enough, loyalty enough, honor enough, patriotism enough to live up to their Constitution."[16] In the name of that Constitution, the North successfully suppressed the slaveholder's rebellion. Having contributed to the victory of the Union, this once enemy of the state became a state agent. At the conclusion of the war, Douglass became a patriot, and later he was appointed as a US ambassador. Given that remarkable journey, what are we to make of the nation's ideals?

Frederick Douglass looked at the nation's Fourth of July celebration and called it "hypocrisy," but perhaps it is something worse: consistency. Contemporary scholars have explored the thesis that the freedom phrasings of the founders may be better understood as part of a consistent worldview, not a hypocritical one. When Thomas Jefferson wrote that "all men are created equal," he used a more universal (although explicitly gendered) phrase, but it is clear that he actually meant "all white men." As Edmund Morgan observed, it was racialized slavery and land seizures that made it possible to extend democratic powers to a broader demographic of white people in the first place.[17] The development of popular participation and democratic government proceeded hand in hand with the institutions of slavery and land theft. The move to extend the vote to all adult white males in South Carolina, for example, was thought to be a means to enhance loyalty to slavery and protect the power of the slaveholding elite.[18] Racial slavery and democracy may have been contradictory from Douglass's perspective, but they were mutually reinforcing in Thomas Jefferson's.

These competing (yet equally consistent) visions of the meaning of democracy in the United States and its founding framework persist into the present. On one side, an increasingly diverse political class argues for a vision of a multiracial democracy, while, on the other side, a fascistic movement has risen to its feet, inspired by the ideals of patriarchy and white supremacy and arming itself to return the country to its more explicitly racist past. At the time of writing, elites in both camps claim, with good reason, to be acting in defense of the nation. History reminds us that racists and antiracists can both make legitimate claims to the nation, the flag, the history.

Thomas Jefferson may be the epitome of what is, from our modern vantage point, a persistent national contradiction. No single figure had as long and varied a career or had as much of an impact on our nation's founding documents and principles as did Jefferson. Jefferson waxed poetic about freedom and liberty while personally benefiting from unfreedom and enslavement. He acknowledged the evil of slavery and suggested that preventing emancipation would provoke the "wrath" of God, but didn't believe such a resolution was possible in his lifetime; throughout his life, Jefferson considered himself an enlightened owner of some six hundred human beings.[19] To understand Jefferson in his life process is to understand the nation in its birth process.

Almost three centuries later, so much has changed, but not enough. Many of the questions we ask about Jefferson could meaningfully be asked about ourselves. Although we do not have a system of chattel slavery, we do endure grotesque inequality and murderous state officials and boast the world's largest number of citizens locked in cages—while continuing to celebrate Jefferson's ideals.

Sometimes when I reflect on US history, I imagine how a future generation will look back at him, and at us. From their standpoint, we may seem to be people who, not unlike Jefferson, have lived in a vast prison house of bizarre and unjust privileges and hierarchies. While we puzzle over how Jefferson could have articulated messages of universal freedom while enslaving people, I hope that future generations will puzzle over how we can use words like "freedom" and "democracy" to describe our society, while so many people here enjoy neither.

Even so, a majority of Black political leaders have found the nation, the Constitution, its laws, and its rhetorical resources useful in the fight for a better future. As historian Eric Foner observed, when apartheid was overthrown in South Africa, they had to write a new constitution—but not so in the United States.[20] Here, the Reconstruction amendments were not enforced for nearly one hundred years, but neither were they repealed. Instead of rejecting the nation, everyone from Ida B. Wells and Frederick Douglass in the nineteenth century to Fannie Lou Hamer and Martin Luther King Jr. in the twentieth laid claim to it, with all of its flaws, as a way to get access to a greater freedom, to make withdrawals from the bank of justice.[21] And we must acknowledge: the movements in which they both participated were successful, even if their ultimate aims remain unfinished. For Black people, claiming the nation has been a powerful strategy for transforming it. But it is not the only one.

* * *

There is another strategy, and to many Black people it has been equally compelling: rejecting the United States of America as a national project and refusing to believe it can be reformed. Two of the most prominent and popular examples of this impulse were the Universal Negro Improvement Association (UNIA), organized by Marcus Garvey in 1914, and the Nation of Islam (NOI), founded by Wallace Fard Muhammad in 1930. In both cases, these separatist movements appealed to many thousands of Black people in the United States and beyond, emphasizing Black pride and the need to build up and support Black businesses. Ultimately, each proposed (although didn't realize) the ideal of returning to or creating a separate, Black-controlled sovereign territory. Neither organization can be completely understood by reference to the particulars of its respective doctrines, though. And in both cases, their impact was felt far beyond their memberships.

A political consciousness forged in the fires of transatlantic slavery, the American Revolution, and enslaved peoples' revolts, Pan-Africanism was nurtured in the twentieth century by Marcus and Amy Jacques Garvey and the UNIA, and later by W. E. B. Du Bois, who gave it organization in the form of the Pan-African Congress.[22] The UNIA proposed that Black people return to Africa and fundraised prodigiously for a steamship line that would accomplish the task. Likewise, NOI religious doctrine held that white people were "devils" whose rule over earth was coming to an end, hence the urgency to separate from white-dominated society. And yet, while neither separatist project actually achieved these separations, both were mass movements that succeeded in having a major impact on social movements that secured significant reforms within the United States.

A quick search through the digitized archives of the UNIA newspaper, *The Negro World*, demonstrates that it collected and brought into conversation nearly all of the brightest intellectual and creative minds of what we today call the Harlem Renaissance. Many UNIA members were also, in their day jobs, some of the most militant workers, joining unions and communist organizations in all parts of the country (including the South), and creating the pressure, through mass action, that forced the legalization of collective bargaining and formal recognition of trade unions on a national scale. And while the NOI, as an organization, officially abstained from political activism, it was, in practice, a reliable framework for prisoner activism and, through one of its members, provided essential thought leadership to non-NOI members struggling for civil rights: Malcolm X.[23]

Malcolm X was born Malcolm Little into a Garveyite family. His parents, Earl and Louise, were UNIA activists. Although they lived in the North, Malcolm's family suffered terrible violence at the hands of white supremacists. His father was murdered by white men who beat him up and then left him on streetcar tracks; the streetcar nearly cut him in two. Three of Malcolm's uncles died at the hands of white men as well. White social service agents broke up his family and sent his mother to an asylum. Discouraged by white educators from pursuing his dream of becoming a lawyer, Malcolm turned his intellectual and entrepreneurial energy to petty crime and burglary, which landed him in prison.[24] Is it any wonder that this prisoner would respond positively to the NOI message that white people were devils? Once he left prison, Malcom quickly became a leader within the organization, honing a message that mixed NOI doctrine with sharp political critiques of the United States.

Whereas other Black leaders emphasized the hypocrisy of the United States, Malcolm emphasized its consistency. In Malcolm's hands, the political horizon of separatism, however far away in reality, opened a rhetorical space to make a more radical critique of the United States. That critique included the Democratic Party. Whereas other Black leaders hoped to influence the Democratic Party to support civil rights, Malcolm harbored no such illusions. "The Democrats have been in Washington, DC, only because of the Negro vote," he said in 1964 in his now-infamous speech "The Ballot or the Bullet." "They've been down there four years, and . . . all other legislations they wanted to bring up they brought it up and gotten it out of the way, and now they bring up you. And now, they bring up you. You put them first, and they put you last 'cause you're a chump, a political chump."[25]

Malcolm's separatist stance also made him fearless when it came to speaking out against the US war machine. He wasn't concerned about whether or not he would be perceived as disloyal. Instead, he urged his audience, effectively, to separate from the white man's wars:

> [As] long as the white man sent you to Korea, you bled. He sent you to Germany, you bled. He sent you to the South Pacific to fight the Japanese, you bled. You bleed for white people. But when it comes time to seeing your own churches being bombed and little black girls be murdered, you haven't got no blood. You bleed when the white man says bleed; you bite when the white man says bite; and you bark when the white man says bark. I hate to say this about us, but it's true. How are you going to be nonviolent in Mississippi, as violent as you were in Korea? How can you justify being nonviolent in Mississippi and Alabama, when your churches are being bombed, and your little girls are being murdered, and at the same time you're going to get violent with Hitler, and Tojo, and somebody else that you don't even know?[26]

Stepping into a long tradition of Black leaders who refused to pledge allegiance to the United States, from Martin Delany to Marcus Garvey, Malcolm publicly chided Black activists who referred to "our government" or "our military," language that betrayed their identification with their oppressors. Those who favored integration with a society dominated by white people, he argued, wanted integration into a "burning house." Most famously, he reminded Black audiences of the violent origins of their very presence in North America. "You didn't land on Plymouth Rock," he quipped, "Plymouth Rock landed on you!"

Hope, in Malcolm's speeches and writings, lay not in schemes of American legal reform or national ideal fulfillment, but in global revolution. Like so many other mid-century Black activists, Malcolm was inspired by the successful anticolonial, national liberation movements all over the world, and particularly in Africa. As minister of the NOI, he followed the famous 1955 gathering of representatives from twenty-nine African and Asian nations in Bandung, Indonesia, during which they attempted to pursue a collective "nonalignment" with the competing superpowers, the United States and the Soviet Union. "The black men all over the planet Earth are uniting," Malcolm told members of one mosque, "and all have one object in mind: the destruction of the devil."[27]

When he quit the NOI, in the last year of his life, Malcolm acted on this internationalist perspective, attempting to forge greater connections with nations in the Middle East and Africa and to recruit them as allies in the struggle for freedom in the United States. In two different sojourns overseas, Malcolm operated as an unofficial ambassador of African American struggle. The first trip, funded by his sister Ella Collins, took Malcolm to Egypt, Saudi Arabia, Lebanon, Nigeria, and Ghana.[28] His experiences in Saudi Arabia—making the hajj to Mecca—famously pushed Malcolm to revise his previous categorical denunciations of white people, refining his Pan-Africanist outlook and abandoning the NOI's racial ideology. In Ghana, Malcolm traveled around the newly independent nation with expat Black Americans who were working for the administration of President Kwame Nkrumah. This group included Alice Windom, Vicki Garvin, and Maya Angelou.[29] They introduced Malcolm to Shirley Graham Du Bois, an advisor to the president and the widow of W. E. B. Du Bois. The two of them "fell in love" (in a political sense) with each other right away, and Shirley Du Bois introduced Malcolm to Nkrumah.[30] Under Nkrumah's leadership, Ghana was widely perceived as a model of postcolonial liberation, and a necessary destination for a kind of political hajj for Black activists in the United States—Martin Luther King Jr. attended the country's independence ceremony, and Fannie Lou Hamer, John Lewis, Stokely Carmichael, and many others later visited as well. Malcolm took full advantage of the opportunity to have an audience with Nkrumah, pressing him to formally commit his administration as an ally to the struggle of Black people in the United States. Nkrumah, a graduate of Lincoln University in Pennsylvania, was no stranger to the situation facing Black Americans. He demurred, however, from Malcolm's request, explaining the risks to Ghana that might result from the precedent of interfering in the domestic affairs of another nation.[31]

Undaunted, Malcolm made two other attempts to enlist global allies in the Black American struggle. Once back in New York, Malcolm joined a small gathering of Black leaders in the upstate home of actor Sidney Poitier. Among the eclectic collection of people present were Whitney Young of the Urban League, labor leader A. Philip Randolph, Benjamin Davis from the Communist Party, and artist-activists Ruby Dee and Ossie Davis. There, Malcolm proposed a plan to "internationalize the struggle" by presenting the plight of Afro-Americans to the United Nations (UN). Among those concurring was attorney Clarence Jones, who was authorized to speak for Martin Luther King Jr., who was at the time sitting in a Florida jail cell for protesting segregation.[32]

Malcolm's proposal was not novel but rather was an iteration of a long-standing protest strategy of leveraging international forums to improve the domestic conditions of Black people in the United States. Like Malcolm, veteran activist A. Philip Randolph had converged on a similar plan more than forty years earlier alongside a wide range of thinkers, including Marcus Garvey, Ida B. Wells-Barnett, and William Monroe Trotter. Together, they had all traveled to Paris for the pivotal 1919 Peace Conference to pressure the United States into adopting anti-lynching and antidiscrimination policies, and in Garvey's case, to build a global diasporic politics.[33] In 1946, the National Negro Congress petitioned the then-nascent UN to form a commission to study the social and economic inequality of Black Americans. W. E. B. Du Bois followed up the next year, presenting a collection of essays, "Appeal to the World," to UN representatives in 1947.[34]

A few years later, Black activists more explicitly, and damningly, connected the dots between fascism abroad and at home, building on the precedent set by the Nuremburg Trials and the

United Nations Educational, Scientific, and Cultural Organization condemnation of racism.[35] In Paris in 1951, the Civil Rights Congress, led by two communists, Paul Robeson and William Patterson, presented a 250-page indictment to the UN and boldly titled it "We Charge Genocide." The document opens with the UN's multipart definition of genocide, which includes causing "serious bodily or mental harm to members of a group" and "[d]eliberately inflicting on the group conditions of life calculated to bring about its destruction in whole or in part." The largest section, "The Evidence," is a devastating catalogue of instances of nationwide anti-Black violence, terror, intimidation, and murder. Ninety people from twenty-five states signed their names to the document, including Charlotta Bass (the first Black woman nominated to be the vice president of the United States—by the Progressive Party), and pathbreaking activist Mary Church Terrell.

Holding an original copy of the bound text in my hands at the Schomburg Center for Research in Black Culture, I was pleasantly surprised to see the name of my fellow Voices cast member, Paul Robeson Jr. (along with those of his parents, Paul and Eslanda) as a signatory as well.[36] This was an act of the Black Left, and mainstream organizations did not lend their support. Having long made its peace with anticommunism, the National Association for the Advancement of Colored People (NAACP) publicly dismissed the genocide charge. The UN, already committed to noninterference in US domestic affairs, made sure to ignore the petition entirely. But, as historian David Helps notes in an article challenging the idea that the campaign failed, for many years afterward Black activists such as Audley Moore, the Student Nonviolent Coordinating Committee (SNCC), and the Black Panther Party took up the charge and, like Malcolm, continued to see the UN as an arena for grassroots diplomacy.[37]

One month after the meeting in Poitier's home, Malcolm returned to Cairo to pursue his agenda at a conference of the Organization of African Unity (OAU). The OAU conference was a gathering of official representatives from thirty African nations. Although he represented only two small organizations (one religious, one political, both created and led by Malcolm in the wake of his departure from the NOI), Malcolm was treated like a foreign dignitary abroad, while the US government treated him like an enemy, surveilling his every move.[38] Once again, though, the nations he aimed to enlist did not answer Malcolm's call, beyond a symbolic resolution; once again, the realpolitik of Cold War statecraft trumped Malcolm's idealism. Reflecting on this setback, Malcolm rearranged his schedule to spend the next several weeks meeting with African heads of state individually to press his case.[39]

As Malcolm's spiritual and political horizons widened, he began working out a new way for himself to think about his relationship to the Black freedom struggle in the United States and worldwide, in the context of the Cold War. In September, Malcolm sent some of these thoughts in a letter to Michael Handler, a white reporter for *The New York Times* whom Malcolm had grown to trust. "I am not anti-American, un-American, seditious [or] subversive," he wrote. "I don't buy the anti-capitalist propaganda of the communist, nor do I buy the anti-communist propaganda of the capitalists. I'm for whoever and whatever benefits humanity (human beings) as a whole."[40]

Although Malcolm's political evolution was cut short by assassination in 1965, his attempts to forge international alliances and his willingness to transgress the boundaries of elite consensus about the "national interest" were taken up by two organizations that proved more dynamic than either of Malcolm's: the Student Nonviolent Coordinating Committee and the Black Panther Party. SNCC's heroic work on the frontlines of the fight for democracy in the US South is well-known, but fewer are aware of what historian Dan Berger terms the organization's "unruly internationalism."[41] Like Malcolm, SNCC activists followed the process of national liberation from colonialism closely and began looking to African political actors for ideas and leadership. Whereas previous generations of Afro-Americans saw themselves as more advanced than their African cousins, the decolonization wave of the 1950s reversed the terms of political leadership. "One man, one vote is the African cry," SNCC leader John Lewis declared at the 1963 March on Washington. SNCC's campaign to democratize the Democratic Party came to a frustrating dead end at the party convention in Atlantic City in 1964, when elected delegates from the SNCC-organized Mississippi Freedom Democratic Party failed to be seated, in deference to the all-white segregated delegation. To help the activists heal and recover from this blow, Harry Belafonte began fundraising to send several SNCC members to newly independent Guinea. Like Malcolm, they, too, were able to gain an audience with that country's first president, Sékou Touré, although their agenda was more modest than Malcolm's. Still, it was a life-changing experience and, as Belafonte recalled, it was Fannie Lou Hamer who was "most affected by the trip."[42]

Recuperation and inspiration are one thing, but Black American activists shortly faced a sharper question of their commitment to internationalism and of their relationship to the US state: the US war in Vietnam. The war escalated precisely at the moment that the struggle against Jim Crow claimed victory with the Civil Rights and Voting Rights Acts. The president of the United States, Lyndon Johnson, had forcefully secured passage of these new laws (and had even spoken the movement lyric "we shall overcome" on national television), lending power to the logic of maintaining an alliance with him. "Johnson needs a consensus," as Whitney Young put it. "If we are not with him on Vietnam, then he is not going to be with us on civil rights."[43]

Not everyone took that position. According to historian Keisha Blain, Fannie Lou Hamer boldly spoke out against the war in Vietnam long before many of her peers. In 1965, she sent the president a telegram urging him to "bring the people home from the Dominican Republic and Vietnam," and spoke shortly afterward against the war at a public rally in Washington, DC.[44] Hamer was a lone antiwar voice, but not for long. On the third day of 1966, college student and Navy veteran Sammy Younge Jr. was murdered by a white gas station attendant in Tuskegee, Alabama, in a conflict over a segregated bathroom. In addition to being a student at the famed Tuskegee Institute, Younge was also a member of SNCC, and his murder rocked the organization. Just three days later, SNCC released an antiwar statement—it was the first civil rights organization to do so.[45]

The SNCC statement crossed the boundary of national loyalty in a time of war. Some fifteen months before King broke his own silence on Vietnam, not only did the SNCC statement call for an end to the conflict, but it effectively sided with the official enemy: the Vietnamese. The statement drew a parallel between SNCC's freedom struggle in the US South and the Vietnamese struggle for liberation from colonialism. "The murder of Samuel Young[e] in Tuskegee, Alabama, is no different than the murder of peasants in Vietnam," SNCC declared, "for both Young[e] and the Vietnamese sought, and are seeking, to secure the rights guaranteed them by law." These struggles, they argued, were connected in another way. "In each case," they wrote, "the United States government bears a great part of the responsibility for these deaths." Under pressure from President Johnson, Roy Wilkins, president of the NAACP, used his nationally syndicated newspaper column to condemn SNCC's statement.[46]

The internationalism of Black civil rights activists is rarely part of the stories we tell about them today, particularly in our classrooms. The destruction of the legal edifice of Jim Crow in the US South is now, more than half a century later, claimed as a proud national achievement. But the global perspectives of these Black activists—which led them to question, and in many cases condemn, US imperialism—are less useful for patriotic presentations of Black history. As Dan Berger concludes, SNCC's stance lost them donors and mainstream goodwill, and "an additional cost of SNCC's internationalism may be the domesticating of its memory."[47] Such domestications of Black history are problematic, not only because they are usually intended to serve a narrow definition of the "national interest," but also because they artificially constrain the process of learning about the past. If we really want to understand what inspired and motivated previous generations of Black activists, we need to look beyond the borders of any one nation.

Even amid renewed interest among young people in the Black Panther Party for Self-Defense (BPP), it, too, has been domesticated. In my experience, students are often shocked when they actually read the text of the Panthers' original "Ten-Point Program" because the reforms they proposed seem so modest. The Panthers are best known for their militant approach to stopping policy brutality: by arming themselves in order to police the police. The "safe" elements of their legacy—free breakfast programs, grassroots health initiatives, and their education reform work—are all admirable and can be helpful as entry points to their story. But it was, historian Robyn Spencer argues, their radical internationalism that was a central factor in bringing violent state repression to bear on the group.[48]

From the very beginning, the BPP founders, community college students Bobby Seale and Huey Newton, linked anti-capitalism to revolution in the Third World. Combining radical internationalism with "an equally radical critique of US society," they do not fit comfortably in the Black patriotism framing of history. Like SNCC, the BPP called for solidarity with the Vietnamese resistance fighters.[49] Like Malcolm, the We Charge Genocide petitioners, and so many others, the Panthers sought to use the UN as a platform for advancing their global perspectives, sending delegations to meet with representatives from "revolutionary countries" and demanding that the UN deploy official observers to the "wretched ghettos" of the United States.[50] The Panthers received some material aid from at least two foreign nations: Cuba and Algeria. They also carried out a grassroots diplomacy, meeting with revolutionary activists from Angola, Zimbabwe, Mozambique, and Haiti.[51]

The legacy of the Panthers is far from a settled matter— scholars and activists continue to debate the meaning and lessons of their story. Students, too, may come to a wide range of conclusions from encountering the history of the BPP. Agree or disagree with former Federal Bureau of Investigation director J. Edgar Hoover, his assessment of the Panthers is a remarkable testament to the absurdity of domesticating Black history. Like so many other US officials, he viewed Black protesters as inherently disloyal to the nation. The same man who wiretapped Martin Luther King Jr. also assessed the BPP as the "greatest threat to the internal security of the United States."[52]

The repression of the Panthers had a chilling effect on radical movements but did not eliminate the idea among Black activists that the US government had to be challenged on the global stage, particularly in its new role as a superpower. Afro-American activists continued to forge links with political leaders (official and unofficial) worldwide and often did so under the banner of Pan-Africanism. Pan-Africanism was infused with new momentum in the context of the mid-century rise of national liberation movements on the African continent. By the 1970s, the agenda of Pan-Africanism as a political movement was largely driven by the heads of newly liberated African states.[53]

Although its dominant ideological framework was deeply chauvinist, Black women were increasingly influential thinkers and leaders within Pan-Africanism, in some ways challenging sexist ideas about the ideal of an African woman in revolutionary movements and in some ways conceding to them.[54] Historian Ashley Farmer describes how in the 1970s, Black women asserted themselves on the world stage, rejecting identification with the United States and reshaping Pan-Africanism and themselves in the process. Harlem-based activist Queen Mother Audley Moore had a remarkable political career, spanning Garveyism, communism, the movement for reparations, and Pan-Africanism. She was invited to give the keynote address to the 1972 All-African Women's Congress in Dar Es Salaam, in Tanzania. Moore urged the attendees to unite all over the world to defeat their common foes, which she identified as "United States imperialism, and racism, the most deadly enemies of the liberation forces in Africa today."[55] At the same time, while encouraging participants to reject Euro-US identification and embrace their common identity as Africans, Moore drew on what Farmer describes as "an undifferentiated African past" that "replaced masculine symbols with feminine ones, conjuring visions of African women as queens, merchants, and rulers" and yet was also "peppered . . . with progressive ideas about Pan-Africanism and women's organizing."[56]

For US-based activists, the powerful desire to embrace an African identity not only tended to reinforce conservative, patriarchal ideas, but also made it difficult for US activists to accurately assess political developments on the continent, obscuring class- as well as gender-based conflicts. As historian Russell Rickford notes, the Europe vs. Africa "binary logic" led many US-based Black activists to support regimes that were actually authoritarian, such as that of "Baby Doc" Duvalier in Haiti and Mobutu Sese Seko in Zaire. These leaders actively fostered what Rickford calls a "mystique of blackness" to rationalize antidemocratic moves to strengthen their respective regimes.[57]

For other US activists, encountering African political leaders directly helped them move away from essentialist ideas (cultural or biological) of "Africanness" to embrace more sophisticated ways of understanding the struggle for liberation underway in Africa. In 1972, Panther leader Kathleen Cleaver returned from a visit, concluding that "Africa is a continent riddled by external and internal subversion and division."[58] Thinkers like Kwame Ture (formerly Stokely Carmichael) and Charles Hamilton, meanwhile, developed and popularized the idea that the Black struggle in the United States and national liberation movements in Africa were both anticolonial struggles.

This was an important step forward in attempting to deepen an analysis of anti-Black racism in the United States (in their book, *Black Power: The Politics of Liberation in America*, Ture and Hamilton coined the term "institutional racism"), but some African theorists disagreed.[59] Frantz Fanon's defense of violence in national liberation struggles was well known, but fewer US readers of his book *The Wretched of the Earth* noted that he cautioned against mapping the patterns of anticolonial struggles too neatly onto the US context.[60] Likewise, Amílcar Cabral, leader of the movement that successfully liberated Guinea-Bissau and Cape Verde from Portuguese control, challenged Black activists in the United States to pay more careful attention to the specific dynamics of their own national context.[61]

Black people in the United States have long hoped that our liberation could be achieved within one or more nations of the world. We have thought, at times, that that liberation was at hand, in Haiti, in the United States after the Civil War (and, later, in proposals for a separate territory within the United States), in the Soviet Union, in Ghana, or in other African nations. In each case, we became fierce defenders of what we thought was truly liberated terrain—a place to finally call home. In some cases, we even emigrated, willingly. If we didn't, we defended foreign lands we believed to be truly free as if they were our own. But if nation-building in the abstract has been a powerful lever of motivation and organization, building and enforcing loyalty, citizenship, and borders, in reality, has been, without exception, a bloody business.[62]

In the middle of the twentieth century, the United States government used the context of its conflict with the Soviet Union to police the boundaries of political allegiances: anyone (and often, but by no means exclusively, Black people) were deemed "un-American" or "traitors" or "Soviet agents" if they aimed criticism at US society. In that context, Black activists sometimes hoped that their struggle could be consonant with anticommunism. But in other cases, forced to choose between loyalty to the United States and to Black liberation, we chose Black liberation.

Today, another ideological campaign attempts to put us, once again, in an intellectual straitjacket, confining what can be thought, read, and written to what is acceptably "loyal" to a conservative notion of patriotism. But Black history, like all true pursuits of knowledge, abhors such limitations. One way or another, the outspoken dissidents discussed here—Malcolm X, SNCC, the Panthers, Audley Moore—all exhibited what might be described as unpatriotic behavior, and all espoused internationalist ideas that don't neatly fall into the paradigm of Black History as a Catalog of Contributions to National Greatness. Whatever conclusions one may draw, everyone deserves the opportunity to learn from Black history, not because it can help us rescue the reputation of this nation, but because some of its most inspiring stories invite us to raise our imaginations and aspirations beyond contributing to the competition for supremacy between nation-states.

Through movements such as Pan-Africanism and strategies such as targeting the UN, Black activists in the United States have tried to transcend the limitations of national boundaries. But the UN, as previously noted, has limited power to determine the global order, particularly when it comes to its most powerful member states. We are left with the fact that truly transcending the nation-state is easier said than done. "For all the evil that nation-states have trailed through history in their wake," Barbara Fields once cautioned, "there is as yet no wider basis for democratic politics or even for a struggle to establish democratic politics."[63]

Fields is undoubtedly correct in naming this limitation of our age. It is difficult to imagine a world without nations, and there is a great deal that can be done to improve people's lives by working within and between them. And yet, although our official political arenas are primarily constrained by national borders, the problems facing our species (including climate change and the scourge of war) are not. Still, even granting the current impossibility of global governance, there seems to be a distinct advantage for activists who adopt a global perspective. Noticing the pro-Vietnamese stance of individuals like King and organizations like SNCC, I cannot help but think that there may be historical moments when disloyalty to the nation-state is strongly correlated with the scale of reform activists are able to achieve within it. The unpatriotic stances of some quite salient people in Black history may be distasteful to today's proud patriots, but in many cases, their progressive impact is undeniable. There may be no single Black person in US history who wrestled as deeply with the relationship between Black people and the US nation-state, and was so personally caught on the horns of this historical dilemma, as was Frederick Douglass, when he accepted an appointment as the official US ambassador to Haiti.

* * *

Three quarters of a century before Malcolm X and Fannie Lou Hamer traveled abroad as unofficial ambassadors, gaining audiences with foreign heads of state, Frederick Douglass took up residence in Haiti and dialogued with its president, as the United States of America's official minister to the first free Black nation in the western hemisphere. The fact of his appointment was yet another moment in a truly astounding biography. The nation that had enforced his enslavement, and later hunted him to prevent him from remaining free, now sent him overseas to advance its interests. Through the overthrow of slavery, its legal abolition, and establishment of birthright citizenship, Frederick Douglass was transformed from a relentless critic of the United States to a loyal defender of the Republican Party, one who was optimistic about the nation's prospects in relation to the world. Douglass threw his support behind Ulysses Grant in the 1872 presidential election, and, when Grant prevailed, Douglass was named assistant secretary of the president's commission to study the possibility of annexing Haiti's island neighbor, the Dominican Republic. Before the abolition of slavery, Douglass thought that any attempt to enlarge the territory controlled by the United States could only lead to "more slavery, more ignorance, and more barbarism."[64] In a moment of despair Douglass had even considered leaving the United States to exile himself in Haiti permanently and was making plans to visit when the Civil War caused him to reverse course.[65]

Now, with slavery overthrown, he believed the United States had been reborn, and therefore territorial expansion could be a force for progress, one that could encourage a "multi-form, composite nationality" in place of citizenship defined by whiteness, and, accordingly, "prejudice against color" he hoped, would disappear.[66] With Douglass's track record of loyal service in other federal appointments (including president of the Freedmen's Savings and Trust Company and US marshal of the District of Columbia), newly elected president Benjamin Harrison saw Douglass as a reliable choice in 1889 for the post of US minister to Haiti.[67]

While Frederick Douglass imagined foreign relations (and even, in some cases, annexation) as a means of expanding genuine democracy, promoting human progress, and attenuating racism, the white men in charge of the US government, the military, the business community, and the press had something else entirely in mind. President Harrison made it clear that, to him, naval power was necessary for national prosperity, and the growing US naval fleet would need convenient, strategically located places to refuel. Top of mind for him was the Haitian port, Môle Saint Nicolas.[68] The white press agreed, gushing at the prospects of gaining a foothold in Haiti and exploiting its resources for the benefit of the United States.[69] Citing his work on Grant's annexation commission, some white newspapermen looked favorably on Douglass's appointment. Douglass, meanwhile, complained that such supporters tended to conflate annexation and coercion, emphasizing that he had "never been a coercionist."[70]

And yet, before Frederick Douglass even set foot there, white Americans were laying the groundwork for relations with Haiti based on domination. Just as Douglass began his term as US minister to Haiti, US steamship line owner William Clyde was already lobbying for exclusive trading rights to seven Haitian ports, and he expected Douglass to bring the weight of the US government to bear in the negotiations. Douglass made it clear that he disagreed, and the US press immediately began to express doubts about his competence in the role.[71] Later, Haitian officials became alarmed at the sight of US warships floating off the coast, which they interpreted as a warning. Haitian diplomat Anténor Firmin complained to Douglass about reports in US newspapers that Môle Saint Nicolas had been "promised" to the United States for its exclusive leasing, insisting that such an arrangement would be "an outrage to the national sovereignty of the Republic."[72]

As the pressure mounted, Douglass began to feel that he had become, as he put it, "a servant between two masters."[73] He was committed to defending the Haitian government and advancing what he believed were its best interests, and yet, by December 1890, he had received explicit verbal instructions from the State Department to secure an exclusive lease of Môle Saint Nicolas.[74] Over time, Douglass became "a defender of Haiti more than an advocate for his own country's policy," as historian David Blight put it, "a contradiction he could only sustain for a short while longer."[75] In January 1891, US Navy Rear Admiral Bancroft Ghirardi arrived in Haiti, with instructions from President Harrison to take over the negotiations.

Douglass was advised to "cooperate" with Ghirardi, an untenable setup.[76] Just a few days later, in a truly unique moment in world history, Haitian President Florvil Hyppolite, Firmin, Douglass, and Ghirardi sat down together (with a translator) in Port-au-Prince.

Douglass tried to emphasize the ways in which the leasing of the port could be mutually beneficial and compatible with Haiti's sovereignty. Ghirardi, no doubt accustomed to deference from dark-skinned interlocutors, talked down to the Haitian leaders, emphasizing that the port had been promised, and that "it was the destiny of the Môle to belong to the United States." Ghirardi's obnoxious use of the term "destiny" in this context "surely clanged in the ears of the Haitians as it was translated," Blight wrote.[77] For that brief moment in time, the United States of America was represented, officially, by two men, one white and one Black, each motivated by different visions of the nation they served. That it was not Douglass's vision that prevailed, at home and abroad, is a tragedy of enormous proportions. It should be enough to give any patriot pause.

Black activists in the United States have frequently been inspired by alternative, unofficial ideas about "the national interest." They have also, at times, diametrically opposed or sought to transcend it, emphasizing the interests of the global Black diaspora, or of humanity as a whole, above those of the nation. Often, Black people in the United States who adopt such stances are labeled "un-American," a charge that only makes sense if racists are allowed (as they often are) to define

"American." In a resonant example of this dynamic, when he refused to back William Clyde's demands, Douglass was accused of being "more Haitian than American."[78] As they did in that room in Port-au-Prince some 130 years ago, so too today, two competing visions of the United States sit side by side. One is a vision of a "composite" nation, rejecting prejudice and seeking the kind of freedom that is based on mutual benefit and progress. The other is a vision of society organized by explicit racial hierarchies, where "freedom" means the license to dominate and coerce others, a fantasy of becoming "masters" of others.

In April 1891, Firmin formally declined to lease Môle Saint Nicolas to the United States and concluded the negotiations. Frederick Douglass resigned his post in June. In a series of interviews and articles, Douglass defended his conduct and protested the racism of his erstwhile colleagues. "With a subtlety that hardly made his enemies blink," Blight observed, "Douglass argued that as long as white supremacy lay at the root of American foreign affairs, the country could never achieve noble aims abroad."[79] Recognizing that the opportunity to realize his vision was lost, Douglass once again expressed biting criticism of the United States, returning to the rhetorical style he had displayed in his Fourth of July address, in which our sense of "national greatness" was, as he put it, "swelling vanity." Douglass forcefully indicted the trend toward greedy, rapacious foreign relations. His words were, like his Rochester speech forty years earlier, all too relevant to what was yet to come for Haiti, Latin America, Vietnam,

Iraq, and many more "shocking and bloody" endeavors dictated by the "national interest" in the twentieth and twenty-first centuries:

> Is the weakness of a nation a reason for robbing it? Are we to take advantage, not only of its weakness, but of its fears? Are we to wring from it by dread of our power what we cannot obtain by appeals to its justice and reason? If this is the policy of this great nation, I own that I was not the man to represent the United States in Haiti. I am charged with sympathy for Haiti. I am not ashamed of that charge.[80]

3

Revolution

Tout Moun Se Moun

AMONG THE MILLIONS OF ITEMS in the collections of the Schomburg Center for Research in Black Culture is a remarkable one-page petition from Savannah, Georgia. According to this document, some unknown number of Savannah's citizens gathered in City Hall on July 2, 1795, to consider the question of revolution. Whether or not to make revolution was not at issue, only how to protect themselves from it. "Whereas from the mischiefs which the people of St. Domingo, and other French islands have experienced from the insurrection of their Negroes and People of Colour," the body of the printed petition begins, affirming "the precautions taken by the people of South Carolina, and of the British West India islands, to prevent the importation or landing of any such Negroes or Mulattoes amongst them." News of the uprising of enslaved people in Santo Domingo had reached their shores, and the citizens feared that human beings would arrive as well and further spread the contagion of revolution to Savannah. Indeed, the petition continues with a warning that it may already be too late. "[A]nd the information the Citizens now assembled have received, that a vessel is now lying at Cockspur, recently from Kingston, with near one hundred Negroes on board, whose landing may dangerous to the inhabitants of this state with the daily expectation of many more." The resolution, adopted by the gathered citizens, determined to bar any ships with "seasoned Negroes, or People of Colour" who have spent one month or more in Caribbean islands or West Florida, from docking and disembarking at all.[1]

This document was brought to my attention by Nicole Daniels, who at the time was working as a curriculum writer at the Schomburg Center. Nicole was gathering unique and compelling items from the archives that middle and high school teachers and their students could study in their classrooms. As a contribution to a curriculum series called Teaching with the Schomburg Center's Archives, this particular document was part of a lesson Nicole wrote on the theme of "Abolition as a Black-Led Movement."[2] She was following in the footsteps of scholars such as Manisha Sinha and other historians who have revised our understanding of the movement for the abolition of slavery.[3] Whereas it has so often been portrayed as an effort led by enlightened white people, recent scholarship reveals that abolition was a multiracial movement in every phase led by Black people, particularly by enslaved people themselves. However, as is often the case in these kinds of historical discussions, it can be extremely difficult to find sources that reveal the voices of enslaved people. Too often, we have to learn to "hear" the voices of Black people and of enslaved people from this period through documents written, ironically, by enslavers and other white people.

Read that way, this particular petition on the part of the citizens of the city of Savannah is not only evidence of Black people's leadership in the struggle for abolition, but locates that leadership, in this moment, in the colony of Santo Domingo (also known by its French name, Saint Domingue). It is, to put it another way, one small window into the global power and significance of what we today refer to as the Haitian Revolution.

The "mischiefs" in Saint Domingue began in 1791 and lasted fourteen years. The enslaved population rose up, overthrew their French masters, and successfully fought off imperial invasions from Spain, England, and again France. In 1804, the self-liberated Black people of Saint Domingue proclaimed a new nation, giving it the name the Indigenous Tainos had used for the island: Ayiti (Haiti). No other revolt of enslaved people anywhere in the world was as successful, and it gave birth to the world's first free Black nation in the western hemisphere.

The citizens of Savannah had good reason to be afraid. The victory of enslaved people in Saint Domingue was an earthquake felt around the world, and the United States was not immune to its tremors. Historian Leslie Alexander has documented how both the Haitian Revolution and, later, the establishment of a sovereign Black nation inspired Black activists and liberation movements throughout the United States.[4] In 1800, for instance, inspired by the events in Saint Domingue,

an enslaved blacksmith named Gabriel Prosser formed a plan
for an uprising in Virginia with several hundred coconspira-
tors but was thwarted by both heavy rain and betrayal. James
Monroe, Virginia's governor at the time (and later the fifth US
president), was right to worry that the Haitian Revolution had
"excite[d] some sensation among our Slaves."[5] In Louisiana
in 1811, over 500 Africans from 50 different nations, led by
a refugee from Haiti, rose up together in an attempt to create another independent Black republic.[6] It was, arguably, the
greatest slave uprising in the history of the United States.[7] In
1822, a large conspiracy for an uprising of enslaved people in
South Carolina, led by Denmark Vesey, also gathered momentum, and was also betrayed from within. At trial, leaders of
the plot testified that Vesey had promised supporters that "St.
Domingo and Africa would come over and cut up the white
people if we only made the motion first."[8] For the enslaved, the
Haitian Revolution was a ray of hope, a beacon of freedom in
an unfree world.

* * *

The theme of this book is that the study of Black history
troubles two concepts that are central to our collective identities: race and nation. It also helps us make sense of moments of revolution, when everyday life and relationships are
transformed, and what seemed impossible suddenly becomes
possible. Often, the most expansive possibilities are violently
crushed; yet sometimes there are victories, born of a revolu-

tionary process, that endure. The story of the Haitian Revolution, which on first glance appears to be a simple triumph of Black slaves over white slave owners on one small island, shows the incredible potential of Black people's movements for self-emancipation to transform the world, even as it serves as a reminder of the limitations of achieving liberation within a world of competitive nation-states. The simplistic description of the revolution provided here glosses over the messiness of the actual events; all Black people in Saint Domingue did not line up on the same side in the struggle, although most (but not all) white people did. In the end, the Black-led revolution chose an Indigenous (not an African) name for their new nation, a rejection of the legacy of European colonialism and an embrace of a new identity connected to the island's Indigenous inhabitants. Their constitution, the first in the world to abolish slavery, also aimed to rewrite the rules of race that had dominated their world.

Looking more closely at the Haitian Revolution forces us to abandon myths of the founding (and especially, the founders) of the United States. Although we educators often reach for stories from Black history that can safely be claimed as proud contributions to US history, the Haitian Revolution cannot serve that function. Rather, the opposite is the case: the Haitian Revolution is an embarrassment to the idealistic view of the Revolution of 1776. We could go further: Arguably, the authors of our contemporary, expansive conception of liberty in which each person counts as an actual person are the Haitian revolutionaries, not the North American ones.[9]

The Haitian Revolution deserves more attention in our classrooms. Although the outlines are heroic and inspiring, the more we wade into the details, the more a messier, complicated history comes into view.[10] Despite the revolutionary and transformative fact of winning a free Black nation, the process of forging that new nation was filled with internal tension and conflict. Haiti, like all countries on the globe, was not a naturally occurring phenomenon; it had to be molded into a nation, which meant that not all people's visions of what independence could mean were treated equally.

Whatever their internal disagreements, the self-liberating people of Saint Domingue had little time to sort them out. From the moment the revolution broke out, the most powerful nations on earth at the time were determined to stop it. When they could not stop it, they lied about it. When the people of Saint Domingue proved the lies wrong and successfully established a new nation, the global powers did everything in their power to punish and impoverish the new nation. It is a truly remarkable (yet not often remarked) fact of global history that the two nations whose self-understandings are the most bound up with ideals of individual freedom and liberty, France and the United States, did the most to prevent individual freedom and liberty from existing in Haiti.

* * *

The position of the French colony of Saint Domingue in the late eighteenth and early nineteenth centuries may be difficult

to appreciate in the twenty-first. Today, Haiti rarely dominates
the headlines of the global north except as a site of tragedy
and suffering. But at the same moment that revolutions were
stirring in France and North America, Saint Domingue was a
place of tremendous wealth. The explosive demand for sugar
and coffee stimulated by and in turn stimulating the new industrial ways of working meant that the idyllic island where,
three hundred years earlier, Christopher Columbus had first
reached the so-called New World was producing both more
sugar than all of the other leading exporters combined, as well
as half of the world's coffee. Profits from the labor of enslaved
people in Saint Domingue made other people's fortunes all
over the Atlantic world, and the legacy of that wealth is all
around us, from the Eiffel Tower in Paris to Citigroup in the
United States.[11] It was, as one author concludes, "the richest
piece of territory in the world."[12]

"How could anyone seriously fear such a wonderful colony?" the Caribbean scholar and activist C. L. R. James wrote
in *The Black Jacobins*, one of the most compelling and enduring narratives of the revolution. "Slavery seemed eternal and
the profits mounted. Never before, and perhaps never since,
has the world seen anything proportionally so dazzling as the
last years of pre-revolutionary San Domingo."[13] The success
of the colony led the white colonists, not unlike their North
American counterparts, to complain of "taxation without
representation" back home in France.[14] The United States and
the French colony were linked by surging commercial success; the United States had about five hundred ships involved

in trading with Saint Domingue at the time of the revolution, amounting to roughly 16 percent of all US exports.[15] And yet, James wrote, "With every stride in production the colony was marching to its doom."[16]

That doom was made, in part, by the extreme violence inflicted on the enslaved population. The enslavers favored working people to death rather than providing for them in a manner that would allow their population to increase through natural reproduction; indeed, there was no financial incentive to check the sadism of the masters. If anything, the profit motive encouraged it, and the society grew to embrace a violent ethos. For entertainment, colonists would watch enslaved people burn alive, have their bones broken one at a time, or their bodies exploded from the inside with gunpowder—"a little powder in the arse," as it was known.[17] "Is there anywhere in this world or any other," Haitian author Baron de Vastey wondered, "a race of executioners destined to torture human beings? Are the ex-colonists, here on earth, what the demons are in hell?"[18] In such a society, the enslaved would never win freedom through reform. Freedom required revolution.

As a consequence of this morbid arithmetic, the arrival of revolution was hastened by the resulting demographics: the majority of enslaved people at the end of the eighteenth century in Saint Domingue were African born.[19] The importation of kidnapped human beings reached its peak in 1790, just one year before the revolution began. These people were strangers to each other; they comprised more than a dozen different culturally and linguistically distinct African groups in the colony, including Arada, Kongos, Ibos, Nagos, and Bambara.[20] Kongos, the largest group, may have been up to 60 percent of the population.[21] Kongos, in particular, historian John Thornton noted, came to Saint Domingue with extensive experience in both political and military conflicts in their homeland. "The military experience of many slaves," Thornton wrote, "may well explain the striking military success the rebels enjoyed in the early days of the revolution."[22]

These Kongolese war veterans also brought to Saint Domingue their experience in political struggles. Although the idiom of Kongo ideology was royalist, the questions of the nature and limits of leadership were extensively debated and fought out in civil wars, with different positions—ranging from what Europeans would understand as "republican" and "absolutist" positions—both able to claim deep legacies in Kongolese history and culture to support their views.[23] So, while it is certainly true that the rebels of Saint Domingue exploited the opportunity for change opened by the revolution in France, and while a minority of leaders followed events and ideas in France closely, the majority of Saint Domingue's revolutionaries brought their own political ideas to bear on their predicament. "Kongo," Thornton concludes, "might be seen as a fount of revolutionary ideas as much as France was."[24]

Comprehending the enormity of this social gulf between the leaders and the majority is crucial to understanding the society that emerged from the revolutionary process. In *The Haitians: A Decolonial History* (recently translated from French to English), Jean Casimir, a professor at the State University of

Haiti and a former ambassador to the United States, challenges many common ways of thinking and speaking about the Haitian Revolution. He argues that viewing Haiti favorably as a "Black republic" is problematic, for example, because it adopts the color scheme of the European colonists, who assumed that all of the people they kidnapped and brought to Saint Domingue from Africa were essentially the same as "Black" people everywhere else in the world.[25] He further argues that referring to the Haitian Revolution as the "first successful slave revolution" also concedes too much—namely, it concedes that the colonist-assigned status ("slave") of the people who made the revolution is the most important way to understand who they were and what they accomplished.[26]

Instead, Casimir refers to the enslaved people of Saint Domingue as "captives." Building on the work of other scholars who note that the majority of people working on the island in 1793, the people who made the revolution, were born in Africa, Casimir challenges us to consider the developments from their perspective. They were swept from their homelands and thrust into a bewildering and cruel environment where none of the laws, rules, or traditions they knew applied. And, although they were surrounded by strangers, within the lifetime of a single generation (given the mortality rate), the strangers found a way to join together, rise up, and overthrow the cruel society. That, Casimir notes, is completely different from what happened in other colonial societies, where plantation life was endured by generations of people, who became genuine creoles and knew nothing but life on those plantations. The newly arrived Africans in Saint Domingue, by contrast, could imagine that their home societies were intact, that "their gods [were] alive . . . [and therefore] victory [was] possible."[27] They never had time to internalize their colonized status as an identity (whether "Black" or "slave"), nor did they internalize the French ideals or worldview.[28]

Accessing the views of these African revolutionaries is challenging. Here again, we encounter the silence of the archives, which, by their nature, favor those who have historically controlled the production and storage of documents. We have more access to the conceptions of liberty held by Thomas Jefferson, an enslaver, than we do to nearly any contemporaneous enslaved person fighting for their own liberty anywhere in the Atlantic world. The enslaved people of Saint Domingue had little opportunity to record their ideas, their ideals, or their organizations. We are left with fragments of their voices, corroborated by oral histories and white people's documents. Years after the fact, for example, various participants related the story that the initial uprising was inaugurated one evening in August 1791 by a West African religious ceremony in Bois-Caiman involving animal sacrifice and a blood oath, but the precise role of spiritual frameworks in uniting the rebels, from where I sit, is difficult to know.[29] We do know that the African captives of Saint Domingue "thrust in a common, hellish circumstance" forged something new: a culture that united them and allowed them to endure and prevail through a protracted struggle against all of the European powers.[30]

* * *

I have never been to Haiti. My earliest political education, however, came from the opportunity, as a college student in the mid-1990s, to organize US residents in support of Haitian activists who were opposing yet another US occupation of their country. I was quite moved by a speech given by a representative from the Mouvement Paysan Papaye (Peasant Movement of Papaye) at an event I helped organize at my university. At that time, I understood Haiti as an oppressed nation, but I didn't think of it as a place where people had done something important to transform the world.

It wasn't until a few years later, when I first read *The Black Jacobins*, that I started to perceive Haiti differently, albeit still from afar. In such a state of ignorance, not able to read or understand Kreyòl, each new piece of information, each new conversation with someone who knows more, particularly from the Haitian perspective, fills out major gaps in my understanding. I grabbed the opportunity, recently, to sit in a lecture on the Haitian Revolution, and I was furiously scribbling notes to keep up with recommended books that the speaker, professor Vanessa Valdés, shared with a group of high school teachers assembled for the occasion in a summer educator residency program at the New York Public Library.[31] Some titles I knew and had read, but several others were completely new to me, including Casimir's book *The Haitians*.

When I began to read *The Haitians*, I noted that I was having an emotional response to Casimir's analysis, particularly in his discussion of the revolution's most renowned leader, Toussaint L'Ouverture. It's that tightness in the chest you get when you learn that a hero you revered was actually a flawed human being. I had to temper my pride in L'Ouverture to gain a deeper understanding of the revolution.

Ever since I first read *The Black Jacobins*, I have revered Toussaint L'Ouverture and relished seeing his name pop up in literature and popular culture. And rightly so. His name is synonymous with the Haitian Revolution, and, as its most preeminent leader, he leaves behind a significant literary legacy. His journey from a slave plantation to becoming a leader of the world's most successful rebellion against slavery to death in a French prison is one of the most incredible stories of the modern world. Born to African parents in Saint Domingue as Toussaint Breda, he spent half of his life in slavery, although he was favored with lighter duties (primarily tending to livestock). In about the third decade of his life he was freed and became a small-scale land and slave owner.

For the first two years of the uprising, Breda played a role in developing and spreading it, then in 1793 made a bid for greater leadership. He began calling himself "L'Ouverture" ("the opening") at some point during this period, and introduced himself that way in a remarkable public proclamation issued to "Brothers and Friends" on August 29 of that year. First, he called on his audience to remember Vincent Ogé, who had attempted a previous insurrection in 1790 and was murdered by the colonial authorities the following year. He continued, "I am Toussaint L'Ouverture; perhaps my name has made itself known to you. You know, brothers, that I have undertaken this vengeance, and that I want liberty and equality to reign in St-Domingue." To achieve this, he called for his people to stop fighting each other and to unite. "Equality cannot exist without liberty," he wrote, "[a]nd for liberty to exist, we must have unity."[32] He was right. France, Spain, and England were already vying for control of different factions of the uprising and benefited from disunity among the insurgents. Although at the time of his proclamation L'Ouverture was officially aligned with Spain and in revolt against France, he was already charting an independent course of action, with liberty as an aim and unity as the means to achieve it.[33]

From that bold declaration, L'Ouverture never wavered on the need for liberty. Although he is widely remembered as the father of Haitian independence, he never explicitly declared national independence as a goal; rather, he mostly allied himself with France, while remaining open to other strategic allegiances. To restore control of the colony, and in the context of the rise of radical Jacobins in the metropole's own revolution, France officially abolished slavery in the colony in 1794. At this point, L'Ouverture abandoned his alliance with Spain and switched back to the side of the French, successfully led the expulsion of Spanish troops from the island, and then turned his attention to fighting the British invaders. For the rest of his life, L'Ouverture wrote and spoke as a loyal citizen of France.

In 1801, L'Ouverture, having defeated a rival military leader (Rigaud), took over the Spanish side, making himself master of the entire island. He convened an assembly to formulate a new constitution. It did not assert a new national identity—rather, it proclaimed new ideals for Saint Domingue as a colony of France. Title 2, Article 3 stated: "There cannot exist slaves on this territory, servitude is therein forever abolished. All men are born, live and die free and French."[34] Not a single formerly enslaved person was among those who participated in the assembly. Still, the document, released in June of 1801, was the first modern constitution in the western world to articulate a universal right to freedom from slavery.

When Napoleon took power in France in 1802, he declared himself emperor and decided to reestablish slavery in the colonies. French forces succeeded in doing so in Guadeloupe that same year, and when French troops arrived in Saint Domingue, L'Ouverture's forces fought them bitterly. On his orders, entire cities were burned to the ground to prevent them from being conquered by the French invaders. Unfortunately, L'Ouverture exposed himself in an attempt to parlay with the French and was captured. Before being whisked onto a boat sailing for France, L'Ouverture famously said: "In overthrowing me, you have cut down in Saint-Domingue only the trunk of the tree of liberty of the blacks; it will grow back from the roots, because they are deep and numerous."[35] In France, he was transferred to a remote prison in the mountains where, exposed to the elements and malnourished, he died.

L'Ouverture was correct. As a result of the French reinvasion, the war in Saint Domingue was transformed. What began as a struggle for an expansive conception of French citizenship turned into a revolution for independence from France. In defeating repeated military invaders, abolishing slavery, and building up an administrative state, L'Ouverture had in fact, true to his adopted name, created an opening for Haitian independence, a victory he didn't live to see. His successors, led by Jean-Jacques Dessalines, repelled the French one more time and, in January of 1804, declared a new nation with a new name: Ayiti.

The new nation was split. The people whose names we know—L'Ouverture, Dessalines, Christophe, and so on—were people who only knew life in the colony. Unlike the African captives, those who seized positions of military and, consequently, political leadership, were creoles (and a few ex-slaves) oriented toward making their way within a European-style, colonial society. They spoke French. They didn't want to end the plantations; in fact, some of them owned plantations, or wanted to. They admired the European powers and looked down on what, to them, seemed like the strange, savage ways of the African captives. This orientation explains the continuity between their attempts to gain equality for themselves within the colonial framework and their later attempts to forge an independent nation. In both phases of their political efforts, they assigned the African captives the same role—plantation workers, producing commodities for export to a global market—and never contemplated that they could or should be people whose consent was necessary to form the basis of a government.[36]

Casimir is not alone among Haitian scholars in this assessment of how Haiti's divisions emerged from the revolution. "From 1789 to 1820, the Haitian people enacted the only great

slave revolution in the entire memory of humanity," wrote the
Haitian scholar Michel-Rolph Trouillot in his first book (published in the language of the majority, Haitian Kreyòl). "But
during those same thirty years or so, a native-born class turned
its back on the people," and, he added, "they overturned the
revolution."[37] Their vision of a society based on active citizenship for a few, and plantation labor for a powerless majority,
was not unique. In this way, despite overturning the global
color line, the outlook of the people whom Casimir calls the
"Haitian oligarchs" was not entirely dissimilar, he concludes,
to that of the founders of the United States.[38]

In this reading, L'Ouverture, like all heroes in history, appears far more complicated upon closer inspection. When he
gained control of the island, L'Ouverture welcomed some former planters back to Saint Domingue, became a plantation
owner himself, and used troops to repress rebellious workers
who feared he was returning them to slavery.[39] L'Ouverture's
dictum echoed Booker T. Washington in its praise for the
market system: "The liberty of the blacks can be consolidated
only through the prosperity of agriculture."[40] To overcome the
majority's resistance to plantation agriculture, L'Ouverture attempted to militarize plantation production.[41] Dessalines, his
successor, was part of a new class of landowners of African descent. Formerly enslaved people now entered a labor struggle
against former plantation managers and owners.[42] For the new
political class, the revolution was mainly about replacing the
leadership of the plantations, but, as historian Laurent Dubois
wrote, "not necessarily replacing the plantation system itself."[43]

I remain in awe of Toussaint L'Ouverture, his remarkable rise, and his inspiring leadership of one of the greatest social struggles the world has ever seen. But I understand now that his vision of what liberty would mean in Saint Domingue was more or less similar to the kind of market-oriented national regimes that his enemies were consolidating in Europe and building anew in North America. L'Ouverture could, however, imagine what those leaders could not: a world of global commerce without racialized slavery, in which Africans and their descendants participated as political and social equals.

* * *

The whole world knew that the stakes of the Haitian Revolution came down to one word: *liberty*. In fact, as information spread by ships throughout Atlantic ports, the idea that the revolutionaries of Saint Domingue were fighting for liberty was widely and explicitly acknowledged. In Jamaica, the news from Saint Domingue, one white man noticed, had made the Black people "so different." He complained that "the Ideas of Liberty have sunk so deep in the Minds of all the Negroes, that whereever the greatest Precautions are not taken, they will rise."[44] Likewise, a British general, sent to crush the Haitian revolution, defined his goal as preventing the spread of "the wild and pernicious Doctrines of Liberty and Equality."[45]

The Haitian Revolution embarrasses attempts to remember US founders as unequivocal lovers of liberty. Thomas Jefferson, author of the phrase "all men are created equal," was afraid of the Haitian Revolution. "St. Domingo has expelled all it's [*sic*] whites, has given freedom to all it's [*sic*] blacks, has established a regular government of the blacks and coloured people," he complained, "and seems now to have taken it's [*sic*] ultimate form, and that to which all of the West India islands must come."[46] In 1799, he wrote to US President Adams, warning that continuing commerce with L'Ouverture would spread the revolution: "We may expect therefore black crews, and super-cargoes and missionaries and thence into the southern states," he fretted. "If this combustion can be introduced among us under any veil whatever, we have to fear it."[47] In his mind, a US military intervention on the island was the answer; it could "re-duce Toussaint to starvation" and thus promote peace among European powers.[48]

Among the so-called founders, Jefferson was not alone. Madison and Hamilton both expressed concern about the up-rising in Saint Domingue.[49] Alexander Hamilton supported gradual emancipation for enslaved people in New York State but characterized the immediate self-emancipation taking place in Saint Domingue as "calamitous."[50] The nation's first president, George Washington, expressed concern about "a spirit of revolt among the Blacks" and said that the start of the uprising was "both daring and alarming."[51] Washington wrote to a French minister that the "United States are [well disposed] to render every aid in their power . . . to quell 'the alarming insurrection of Negroes in Hispaniola.'"[52]

Over nearly a two-year period (1791–1793), US officials sent $726,000 to Saint Domingue to support enslavers in suppressing the revolution.[53] It was, historian Timothy Mat-thewson writes, "the only occasion that the United States attempted to suppress a foreign slave revolt." The reason was simple: Saint Domingue was unlike any other island. Its proximity to the United States, its wealth, and its influence in the United States, the Caribbean, and the wider Atlantic world were unparalleled. "No other island could threaten the United States in a wide variety of ways that Saint Domingue did. Washington, Jefferson, and Hamilton could ill afford to acquiesce in the destruction of Saint Domingue's plantation society because of the multiple threats such an event posed to American interests, and," he concludes, "because they did not like slave revolts."[54]

One measure of the global importance of Saint Domingue is the sheer scale of human resources the great powers deployed to capture it. Five long years after invading, Britain withdrew from the island in defeat in 1798. The crown spent more re-sources trying to claim Saint Domingue than they did trying to keep their North American colonies. "More British sol-diers fought and died in the failed attempt to take over Saint Domingue," journalist Howard French observed, "than at the hands of America's revolutionary army two decades earlier."[55] Napoleon, for his part, explained his decision to re-enslave Saint Domingue in racial terms: "I am for the whites because I am white; I have no other reason, and that one is good. How could one grant freedom to Africans, to men who have no civ-ilization, who don't even know what a colony is, what France is?"[56] At least fifty thousand French soldiers, including eighteen military generals, died trying to reclaim the territory. Napoleon, like King George III, had drastically underestimated the Africans defending the island.[57]

At the same time, because the Haitian Revolution occurred in the context of a complicated game of international rivalry and competition between France, Spain, England, and the newly formed United States, Saint Domingue was never completely isolated economically.[58] The United States in particular saw an interest in both suppressing the uprising and benefiting from France's loss of its most valuable colony. When L'Ouverture moved to take control of the entire island of Hispaniola in 1801, for example, he did so with assistance from the US Navy.[59] Although the United States did not formally recognize Haiti until two decades after its independence, northern American newspapers quickly began identifying the new nation by its new name, and the US Congress explicitly discussed the fact that continued trade ran the risk of "tacit" recognition.[60] In the 1820s, US trade with Haiti surpassed its trade with Russia, Prussia, Sweden, Norway, Denmark, Spain, Portugal, Italy, and Malta combined.[61]

In truth, the Haitian revolutionaries played a major, and underrecognized, role in shaping the newly formed United States of America. Napoleon dreamed of a French empire on the North American mainland, but the Haitian Revolution forced him to abandon that ambition.[62] Were it not for the Haitian Revolution, the Louisiana Territory would not have been for sale. It was the Haitian Revolution that enabled Jefferson to seal the deal, acquiring 530 million acres for just $15 million, doubling the size of the United States overnight. Hamilton acknowledged that "to the courage and obstinate resistance made by its Black inhabitants are we indebted for the obstacle which delayed the [French] colonization of Louisiana."[63] Of course, what Jefferson really purchased, historian Annette Gordon-Reed noted, "was the right to contend with the various Indigenous people who had their own claims to the land."[64]

Besides the geographic transformation, there is another debt. For all its flaws, it was Haiti, not France or the United States, that pioneered the ideal of universal liberty.[65] The concept is expressed in Haitian Kreyòl as *tout moun se moun* ("every person is a person").[66] The French and American revolutions are widely remembered as advancing modern notions of personal liberty and human freedom. In reality, they both were revolutions rooted in a cramped vision of liberty and freedom as the exclusive preserve of white people and made possible by the unfreedom of enslaved and colonized people, for whom the lofty rhetoric of rights was never intended. There were people in France opposed to slavery, but they favored gradual emancipation. The Haitian Revolution put such people "in a bind: the group's careful plans for reform, too much for many whites," Dubois observed, "were also clearly too little for the slaves."[67] The self-emancipation of people in Saint Domingue "was the ultimate test to the universalist pretensions of both the French and the American revolutions," Trouillot wrote. "And they both failed."[68]

* * *

In revolutionary Haiti, the battle between competing visions of what liberty should mean were more or less fought to a draw. The former captives, who had participated in the overthrow of the colonial order and the war for independence, were not so easily corralled into the leaders' ideas of their role in the new nation. The revolution overthrew the old management, and the new management was inexperienced in running an economy and lacked social bridges to the workforce. The new leaders oversaw the towns and the state apparatus, but in the countryside, the rest of the population increasingly controlled their own day-to-day lives. More importantly, even when troops did invade their areas, the sovereign Haitian people cultivated a social space of their own, which they called the *lakou*. It is a complex term, scholar Walter Mignolo explains, which "names the confluence of land (meaning complementarity of life and earth, not a piece of private property) that implies the extended family (not the Christian/bourgeois family and its private property) and spirituality (rather than secular states)."[69]

Furthermore, the captives, as a community, appropriated and revised the Kreyòl language.[70] And they invented a new institution, Vodou, to express their spirituality.[71] The social system that they developed over fourteen years of war was the kind of victory that agricultural people all over the world sought in the face of the growing pressure to prioritize commodity production.[72]

The authorities were powerless to stop the development of what Casimir calls "the counter-plantation."[73] Rather than imagine their future as becoming more like the French, the former captives embarked on "the reverse of the absorption of peasant communities into Western, capitalist industry."[74] Although the new elite imagined themselves as leaders of a society that had been and—they hoped—would continue to be French, Catholic, and based on plantation agriculture, the overwhelming majority of the population, the former captives from Africa, forged an entirely different identity for themselves.

For the European-oriented revolutionaries, meanwhile, citizenship was a double-edged sword. France offered citizenship to free people of color early in the revolution as a way to contain the aspirations of the enslaved population. The revolutionaries responded by trying to transform French republicanism into Black revolutionary abolitionism.[75] When that proved untenable, the revolutionaries fought for independence and established their own nation. But Haitian citizenship, as defined by the new ruling group, was still too narrow to contain the freedom dreams of the liberated majority. They had examples of successful maroon societies in Saint Domingue and their memory of other subsistence cultures in Africa to draw upon when imagining the meaning of postindependence freedom. The result, Casimir argues, was that the newly independent Haiti was born as a "bicephalous state"—a state with two heads, two minds, two worldviews.[76] Eventual Haitian President Jean Bertrand Aristide noted that this pattern endured in the twenty-first century. "More than 200 years later, Haitian identity is still split," Aristide wrote, "with the great mass of the Haitian people on one side, and a small elite who remain identified with today's colonizers on the other."[77]

Haiti's naming may be a product of that tension. Haiti was the only Caribbean colony to change its name in the process of independence.[78] The choice of an Indigenous name, and not an African one, is a puzzle. On the one hand, it suggests an undoing, as Laurent Dubois put it, "not only of French colonialism, but of the whole history of European empire in the Americas."[79] For the new Afrophobic elite, it may have been a choice that aimed to forge a common national identity that was acceptable to both of the new nation's "heads" precisely because it was neither French nor African.[80]

And yet, if the newly born United States of America was to be a "white" nation, the new Haitian elite declared that their nation (despite its new name) would be a "Black" one. Blackness became the official national identity. Eliminating previous distinctions of color, Article 14 of the 1805 Constitution concludes, "Haitians will henceforth be known only under the generic name of Blacks."[81] Famously, the new nation inverted the North American rules of race; it would not be a country in which people sought admission into whiteness. In one fascinating case, hundreds of Polish soldiers who, in the course of war, switched sides and fought for Haitian independence, were also accepted as "Black" in this new racial paradigm.[82] That kind of expansive, political Blackness remains a rich latent possibility for forging a path through the tortured logics of race, moving toward liberation.

* * *

I recently had the good fortune to be able to travel to Paris. I cherished my time there, taking in the architecture, the food, and the language. I clocked many miles of walking almost every day, I visited several libraries, and I landed frequently in the early evenings at a sidewalk cafe, with a glass of wine and a book. The book in my hand was often Casimir's *The Haitians*, and so everywhere I went my sense of awe was tinged with sadness and anger. The more I read, the more I began to see Paris differently. With Haiti on my mind, I thought about how the grandeur of that historic city was wrung from the blood and sweat of French colonies, including Saint Domingue. The story of theft, however, doesn't even end with independence. After Haiti won its freedom, France continued to exploit its former possession. Once free of French control, by any sense of fairness, France owed the Haitian people reparations. Yet, France never paid reparations to Haiti. Actually, the opposite occurred. If we are to understand how it is that Haiti's fortunes fell and France's rose, we must face the fact that it is not the result of the cultural qualities or economic prowess of the different people in each place. Rather, the truth is that France refused to allow Haiti's economy to develop. With a gun to its head, it was Haiti who paid reparations to France.

Twenty-one years after declaring independence, French warships armed with five hundred cannons appeared off the coast of Port-au-Prince, threatening to cut off all trade with the young nation. King Charles X of France's emissary, the Baron de Mackau, demanded that Haiti, in essence, pay reparations to France in the amount of 150 million francs, in annual installments. Haitian president Jean-Pierre Boyer, most likely seeing the ransom as preferable to unending warfare with France, acquiesced to the demand. Haiti remained formally free and independent, but in practice, after 1825, it was shackled with a crippling debt, the effects of which are still felt two hundred years later. The very first payment completely emptied the government's coffers. Every subsequent payment was made possible by taking out loans from French banks at usurious rates—as high as 40 percent—pushing the country deeper into debt and making it impossible to spend money to build schools, hospitals, roads, or any kind of infrastructure necessary to the new nation.[83]

In 2022, *The New York Times* published its own research on these payments and their devastating impact on Haitian society. "We found that Haitians paid about $560 million in today's dollars," they wrote.

> But that doesn't nearly capture the true loss. If that money had simply stayed in the Haitian economy and grown at the nation's actual pace over the last two centuries—rather than being shipped off to France, without any goods or services being provided in return—it would have added a staggering $21 billion to Haiti over time, even accounting for its notorious corruption and waste.[84]

Some economists argued that $21 billion is a conservative estimate and think that if Haiti had been able to grow in ways that are comparable to its regional neighbors, the total loss should be calculated as closer to $115 billion.[85] Throughout the nineteenth century, Haiti remained a symbol of freedom, but to many Black Americans, Boyer's concession diminished the Black republic's legacy of resistance and, for a time, undermined their confidence in it.[86] Still, Haiti's status as a beacon of freedom endured, and Black Americans continued to look upon the nation with pride. Not unlike L'Ouverture, Frederick Douglass, too, hoped that Haiti would successfully carve out a lucrative niche for itself in the global marketplace.

The US government had other plans. When the United States invaded Haiti in 1915, it installed a new government and took over the banks. National City Bank (predecessor of Citibank) bought all of the shares in Haiti's national debt so that it could continue the pattern of prioritizing debt repayment over social spending. "From 1825 to 1957," the *Times* explained, "international debt drained an average of 19 percent of the country's annual revenue, and in some years ate up more than 40 percent."[87] As a newly born nation, late arriving to the game of global competition, Haiti started off at a disadvantage and was never allowed to thrive. Indeed, the great powers actively worked to stifle Haiti's development. The violent US occupation further entrenched the gap between the urban elites and the rural majority, and then, tragically, "ruler after ruler" did the same, as Haitian American scholar Gina Athena Ulysse noted, choosing "to concentrate power and develop the capital at the expense of the nation."[88] Too often racism provides a convenient way to understand Haiti's problems as a simple result of the people's shortcomings. In the wake of the 2010 earthquake that devastated the nation, David Brooks wrote that Haitian culture is "progress-resistant."[89] Such racist, culturalist explanations for national poverty (or for national wealth) ignore history. In truth, it is France and the United States that have been the most "resistant" to Haitian progress.

* * *

The Haitian Revolution deserves time and attention in our classrooms. The revolutionaries of Saint Domingue, in the most valuable colony of the world, broke the chains of slavery and set the world on a path to abolition. People all over the world, seeking freedom, had the name "Toussaint L'Ouverture" on their lips. For Black people in the nineteenth century, as historian Johnhenry Gonzalez put it, Haiti in the nineteenth century "was the closest thing to a free country that existed anywhere in the New World."[90] But people who wanted to preserve the status quo looked at the Haitian Revolution with fear and dread. Just as the citizens of Savannah tried to stop the spread of information about the revolution at their ports, today we stop information about the revolution from arriving in our classrooms. What Frederick Douglass said in Chicago in 1893 could be said today, that there was a "deeper reason for coolness" toward Haiti. Simply put: "Haiti is Black, and we have not yet forgiven Haiti for being Black or for the Almighty for making her Black."[91]

The Haitian Revolution, like the height of Radical Reconstruction after the US Civil War, provided a glimpse of an alternative future in which each society might have been remade on the basis of equality, where *tout moun se moun*. In both cases, Black people played a leading role in their own liberation and, in doing so, opened up the possibility of creating a better world for all people. Some even saw the US Civil War as a "second Haitian Revolution."[92] But in both cases, people who wanted to defend the priorities of capitalism and white supremacy prevailed through naked violence to reassert control and squash those dreams of freedom. In both places, elites prioritized reasserting plantation agriculture and commodity production, and Black people's desire to be free of both was violently repressed. The pattern of state violence in both the United States and Haiti has deep roots in racism and profit seeking. For "the two oldest nations in the Americas, born of revolution," Haitian American scholar Mamyrah Prosper and anthropologist Mark Schuller note, those forms of violence are "symptoms of the structural inequalities of racial capitalism."[93]

And yet their revolutions were, in some important ways, very different. Whereas the American Revolution consolidated the system of slavery, the Haitian Revolution destroyed it. Just as the French were perfectly willing to abide the contradiction between their language of *liberté* and the reality of enslavement (and their violent attempts to reestablish it in Haiti), so too were the Americans willing to proclaim the "self-evident" equality of all men while holding millions of them in literal shackles.[94] Furthermore, the heroes of the American Revolution were elites. They were, as Haitian political leader and writer Baron de Vastey wrote in 1816, "white Englishmen, free and propertied, [who] enjoyed their natural civil and political rights" whereas the Haitian revolutionists were "black and enslaved, without country, without property, deprived of their natural rights."[95] As an act of political liberation, and self-organized by enslaved Africans in their own interest, the Haitian Revolution was a more profound rupture from the pattern of the modern world than the American or French Revolutions and was carried out by those with the least access to literacy. It was too radical to be written down in advance, and its most determined agents did not write. "By necessity," Trouillot observed, "the Haitian Revolution thought itself out politically and philosophically as it was taking place."[96]

The histories of Black people's transformative actions during the Haitian Revolution—liberating themselves from enslavement, defeating the strongest European armies to defend their liberty, and forging a new, but deeply divided nation—are worth serious study. But instead of a narrative of Black freedom fighters consistently opposed by violent white supremacists, the popular story (of Haiti, as of the US South) is one of Black people's corruption, laziness, and inadequacy for self-government contrasted to white people's commitment to hard work and steadfast adherence to the ideals of liberty and democracy. Black history shatters those myths. And rather than trapping us inside rigid ideas of race or of nation, these moments of Black-led revolutionary transformation point to alternative, even if not yet fully realized, possibilities.

4

Education

The "Mightier Work" of Reconstruction

WHEN I JOINED THE STAFF of the Schomburg Center for Research in Black Culture, one of my first trips to the Manuscripts, Archives, and Rare Books Division was to view the contents of a single box containing materials related to the Black Panther Party in Harlem. I'd read several books about the Panthers and considered myself knowledgeable on the topic, so I was intensely curious to know what more I might learn from the Schomburg Center's collections. Exploring archives, I have found, is usually an exercise in humility. If reading books can make you feel like an expert, reading archival documents can make you feel like you know nothing. The experience of looking through collections of primary sources can often feel, at least initially, confusing. For the Panthers, the Schomburg Center has just one box. How surprising could it be?

On that spring day, I made my way to the second floor, presented my library card at the desk of the Manuscripts Division, and took a seat. A few minutes later, a librarian set a box labeled "Black Panther Party Harlem Branch files" on the table before me.[1] I opened the box, pulled out a folder, and began gently leafing through the contents. My attention settled on a letter, typewritten on a single page of paper. It was addressed to the Harlem community, with a return address on Seventh Avenue and signed by someone named George M. Miller, announcing the formation of a Black Panther Party in Harlem. Dated August 20, 1966, it begins by explaining that Black people, who comprise 80 percent of citizens in Lowndes County, Alabama, had formed a Black Panther Party, "and they have as their goal nothing less than taking over the County and running it themselves." But, the letter continues, unlike the Democratic and Republican parties, the Panthers, now spreading to several northern cities, would not be a mere "vote-getting machine" but a social movement addressing itself to the needs of Black people.

Although most popular accounts of the rise of the Panthers cite their origin point as the Bay Area in California, I did already know that the Panther logo and party idea started in Alabama. So far, so good. What surprised me was the way the letter proposed to launch the movement in Harlem: It lays out a series of demands to reform Harlem's public schools.

If you do a Google image search for "Black Panther Party," you will retrieve pictures of gun-toting radicals in leather jackets and berets. To their admirers, the Panthers were courageous revolutionaries who dared to police the police (and produced innovative nutrition, public health, and education programs).[2]

To haters, they were dangerous thugs and criminals. But the matter of police brutality, so central to the conception and activity of the party formation in the Bay Area, was not mentioned at all in this letter to the Harlem community that I held in my hands. Instead, the energy of this Harlem Panther organization would be targeted at the Board of Education. They vowed to "shut down the public schools in Harlem one by one" if their demands weren't met. What were the demands?

1. African and African American history and culture taught in all Central Harlem Public Schools.

2. Black principals in all Central Harlem Public Schools.

3. Change the names of the public schools so that they reflect the history and achievements of OUR PEOPLE.

This vision of a Black Panther Party focused on school reform was surprising. But even more so was the sense of disorientation I felt when I took a closer look at the date in the top right corner: August 20. I knew that the idea for the Black Panther Party had traveled from Lowndes County to Oakland, where Huey Newton and Bobby Seale reworked it into a new model that captured the imagination of Black people nationwide, and later, globally. But that formation came together in October of 1966—two months after the announcement of a party of the same name in Harlem.[3] Suddenly, this document took on a whole new relevance in my mind. Rather than a Harlem organization trying to branch off from the Oakland party, or develop in imitation of it, here was evidence of young Black activists taking up the Black Panther Party idea directly from Alabama, just as Newton and Seale would soon do, too, and applying it in their own way in their own place.

After that afternoon in the archives, my curiosity about this Harlem party led to more digging, and more learning. I spoke to historian Donna Murch and consulted a book chapter she wrote on the way the Panther idea traveled from Alabama.[4] I learned that there were actually two Black Panther Parties in Harlem; the first, initiated by young radicals and taking inspiration from the battle for democracy in Alabama, produced the letter that I found, but it was quickly overshadowed by the second: the Oakland Party. The second Harlem Black Panther Party took shape as a branch of the party for self-defense started by Seale and Newton in Oakland. It gained notoriety for a protracted and successful campaign to defend twenty-one of its Harlem members from charges of planning bombings and long-range rifle attacks on police and other targets—precisely the kind of conflict that consumed its parent organization in the Bay Area. The story behind this mysterious letter was becoming clearer, and I thought of Robin D. G. Kelley's caution in *Freedom Dreams*, to avoid evaluating every movement by whether or not it "wins."[5] Here was an idea, a vision, a freedom dream, that was formalized and announced, but didn't endure, at least not in the way the dreamers imagined. But I still wanted to know why, given that police brutality was a serious problem in both Oakland and in Harlem, the Harlem activists had initially chosen one path while those in Oakland chose another. Why the emphasis on education?

Later, in preparation for a summer institute for teachers at the Schomburg Center, another piece of the puzzle fell into place. This institute, codirected by education historian Ansley Erickson and myself, offered twenty-five middle and high school educators from all over the United States the chance to dive deeply into the history of education-related activism in Harlem, from the 1920s through the 1970s.[6] One of our institute's guest lecturers was longtime educator, mathematician, poet, and activist Sam Anderson. I talked with Sam about his journey from growing up in Brooklyn to studying at Lincoln University (one of the nation's oldest HBCUs) to joining the Student Nonviolent Coordinating Committee, and many different organizations and manifestations of the Black Power and Black Arts movements. When those activists—whom I would later learn were teenagers—sat down, in August of 1966, to type out their announcement for a new Black Panther Party in Harlem, Sam was one of them.

Sam confirmed the basic story I learned from Donna Murch—that this early Panther formation didn't last, was outshone by and ultimately absorbed in the meteoric rise of the West Coast organization—and he added some new details. The letter, he told me, was typed out in the apartment of Harlem-based Japanese American activist Yuri Kochiyama. Kochiyama, whose family suffered internment during the Second World War, was a trusted friend and comrade of Malcolm X (famously photographed cradling his head as he lay dying after assassins pumped his body with bullets in Harlem's Audubon Ballroom) and has remained since then a potent symbol of the promise of Black-Asian solidarity.[7] The young would-be Harlem Panthers chose Kochiyama's apartment for the simple reason that she owned a typewriter and allowed them to use it. Sometimes that simple gesture alone from an elder is powerful: giving young people space and resources to dream their own dreams and write their own stories.

To the question of why they chose to focus their initial efforts around education, Sam replied simply that it was the issue for which there was already the greatest activist momentum in Harlem. That the terrain of education activism would have that status in Harlem was, in part, what we were exploring in our summer institute, connecting dots between Ella Baker's educational work with young people at the 135th Street branch of the New York Public Library (today known as the Schomburg Center) in the 1930s, to Mae Mallory's leadership of a legal campaign by Black parents in the 1950s to challenge what they considered inferior schooling in Harlem, to the little-known 1964 citywide boycott against segregation in New York City's schools.[8] Half a million students participated in the boycott, making it the single largest action in the traditional "civil rights movement" timeline.[9]

When I began teaching elementary grades in Harlem's public schools in 2003, the public discourse about my mostly African American students and their parents was that they were disinterested in education and were failing to take advantage of the educational opportunities before them. I may have been ignorant of the history of educational activism in Harlem at the time, but as a student of Black history in general, I knew that the opposite was true: In North America, Black people have consistently been obsessed with education. This centuries-long struggle for learning and liberation runs like a red thread throughout Black social movement history. The popular wisdom about my students and their parents was a lie, serving to cover the shameful truth: despite Black people's unrelenting efforts, our society has consistently attempted to thwart our access to literacy, to stifle, contain, and constrain it.[10] Perhaps the clearest example of this historic dynamic is to be found in what was also the most consequential and pivotal moment for the nation as a whole: Reconstruction.

* * *

It matters where a story begins, and I think we learn something important about our current moment by starting our story with Reconstruction. To say that we are living in the aftermath of the violent overthrow of Reconstruction shifts our attention to the unfulfilled promise of that period and offers it as a yardstick to measure our progress or lack thereof in the present. It is more commonplace, understandably, to reflect on a goalpost from the more recent past. In the field of education, for instance, instead of seeing ourselves as post-Reconstruction, we more often perceive ourselves to be post-*Brown*.

For most of the last half century, Black people's historic struggles for learning and liberation have been framed as living up to, or failing to achieve, the great promise of the Supreme Court's famous *Brown v. Board of Education* decision that racially segregated schooling is unconstitutional.[11] But *Brown's* legacy is more complicated than most people realize, beginning with the fact that many of the nation's largest school systems remain, decades later, stubbornly segregated and unequal (critical race theory, a phrase which today operates more as a political bogeyman, was created by legal scholars in the post–civil rights movement era to grapple with the contradiction between the legal abolition of discrimination and its persistence.)[12] And even where desegregation did succeed, Black people did not always experience that process as an improvement. In *Brown's* wake, white politicians charged with fulfilling its mandate decided that Black educators and the institutions they nurtured were superfluous. As a consequence, Black people often experienced desegregation as disempowering, especially as their children were hurled into hostile schools where their inferiority was assumed by educators who didn't know them.

Ironically, it was precisely upon the matter of "inferiority" that the *Brown* decision turned. The nation's highest court decided that segregated schooling created a "sense of inferiority" for Black students and was therefore in violation of the Constitution's promise of equal protection by law, guaranteed by the Fourteenth Amendment. That same Fourteenth Amendment was the fruit of Reconstruction's radical phase. But after actively working to undermine the Reconstruction Amendments for several decades, the court finally decided to reverse course and uphold them—in a limited way—citing the feeling of inferiority as detrimental to the learning process, and therefore as an injury to the plaintiffs, Black students.

As many scholars have noted, the *Brown* decision was consonant with the United States' shift toward abandoning Jim Crow (in the South) to assert its moral superiority in the context of global competition with the Soviet Union. The Supreme Court's reversal of its own precedent—the 1896 *Plessy v. Ferguson* decision—was part of this new Cold War consensus. Although *Brown* was decided during the Eisenhower administration, the Truman administration, in its last days, weighed in by filing amicus briefs arguing that a pro-segregation decision would have negative international implications.[13] As noted in the second chapter, the Cold War cut two ways for the US Black freedom struggle: on the one hand providing greater leverage for the abolition of Jim Crow, and, on the other, restraining Black activists' more radical, structural (and especially, anti-capitalist) analyses, in favor of an understanding of racism as a problem of psychology and individual prejudice.[14]

Measuring our present schooling systems by the yardstick of *Brown* is, thus, a more limited way to frame our present struggles; measuring them by Reconstruction is another. To do so is to hold ourselves to a higher standard. In this moment in which the idea of "abolition" has gained popularity, revisiting Reconstruction also offers an opportunity to imagine the important work that comes after. If history is a guide, Reconstruction is even more difficult than abolition. Speaking of the post-slavery struggle to define freedom, Frederick Douglass warned, in 1865, that a "mightier work than the abolition of slavery now looms up before the abolitionist."[15] In the US South, Reconstruction was a Black-led revolution to remake the region as a genuine democracy, for the first time. Backed by the northern armed forces occupying the former Confederacy, Black people voted, served on juries, and were elected to public office—six hundred Black people joined southern state legislatures, and sixteen were elected to the US Congress.[16] Black people, with their allies in the Republican Party, opened public institutions such as hospitals and, for the first time in the US South, free public schools.

That the freedpeople focused so intensely on building schools should not surprise us. Black people sought out opportunities to acquire literacy at great risk during slavery. "Because it most often happened in secret," historian Heather Williams wrote, "the very act of learning to read and write subverted the master-slave relationship and created a private life for those who were owned by others."[17] The US Civil War transformed social relations, revealing what had been Black people's secret ambitions to the world. Like every popular revolution, the war was also a mass literacy event.[18] Resources for learning and literacy, cultivated in the shadows during slavery, burst forth in the midst of the conflict, with formerly enslaved people setting up schools for all ages before the fighting was concluded.[19] In the years that followed, Black people and their allies established the first free, tax-supported public schools in the South. In one of the most enduring patterns of US history, non-Black people benefited from what was, essentially, a manifestation of Black Power. Many southern white children went to school for the very first time because of the advocacy of their Black neighbors.

"Public education for all, at public expense, in the South," Du Bois wrote, "was a Negro idea."

* * *

Someone once asked me to name something from Black history that is important but that most people don't know. My reply was twofold: first, that Black people have played a crucial role in defining and attempting to realize the ideals of democracy in this country, and second, that they have also been uniquely focused on pursuing and expanding opportunities for education.[20] Because Black education was criminalized for most of US history, Black people's pursuit of it involved great risk and largely took place in secret. During the Civil War, these efforts came out into the open, surprising white people who observed them. "Few people who were not right in the midst of the scenes can form any exact idea of the intense desire which the people of my race showed for education," Booker T. Washington wrote of the post–Civil War fervor for learning that he witnessed.

> It was a whole race trying to go to school. Few were too young, and none too old, to make the attempt to learn. As fast as any kind of teachers could be secured, not only were day-schools filled, but night-schools as well. The great ambition of older people was to try to learn to read the Bible before they died. With this end in view, men and women who were fifty and seventy-five years old, would be found in the night schools. Sunday-schools were formed

soon after freedom, but the principal book studied in the
Sunday-school was the spelling-book. Day-school, night-
school, and Sunday-school were always crowded, and often
many had to be turned away for want of room.[21]

Believing widely held racist myths that Black people were intellectually inferior, white people who witnessed these developments were surprised, not only by the freedpeople's capacity for
learning, but also their ability to self-organize it. "Many missionaries were astonished, and later chagrined, however," historian James Anderson wrote, "to discover that many ex-slaves had
established their own educational collectives and associations,
staffed schools entirely with Black teachers, and were unwilling
to allow their educational movement to be controlled by the
'civilized' Yankees."[22] To the freedpeople, literacy was power; it
was the power to read and negotiate contracts, to put distance
between themselves and the bitter legacy of slavery, and, importantly, the power to read the Bible for themselves. To secure access to schooling, particularly for their children, the freedpeople
wielded their newfound leverage as wage laborers. In 1866 and
1867, Anderson noted that Freedmen's Bureau officials witnessed
the spread of "educational clauses" in labor contracts between
freedpeople and planters, forcing employers to set aside funds
(and/or materials) for the construction of schools.[23] As Frank
Chase, the Freedmen's Bureau superintendent of education for
Louisiana, described it: "Schools are everywhere springing up
from the soil itself at the demand of those who till it."[24]

We can only imagine what our world today might look
like if these heroic efforts had been allowed to proceed

without opposition. But that's not the past we come from. We are living in the present created by a history in which every forward motion met resistance and pushback. Instead of cheering on the Black-led self-organized education movement, too many white people feared it. The governor of North Carolina, Jonathan Worth, initially supported public education, but in 1865 he reversed himself, worried that once white kids got free schooling, they would "be required to educate the negroes in like manner."[25] With Lincoln assassinated, the Republican Party's attempts to reconstruct the South faced bitter opposition and outright vetoes from President Andrew Johnson, who supported the Thirteenth Amendment (abolishing slavery) but campaigned against the Fourteenth (birthright citizenship, equal protection under the law, and insurrectionists barred from office) and sought to smooth the path of former Confederates back to power in the US South.

Johnson's obstruction forced moderate Republicans to take more drastic action and, temporarily, align with the Republican Party's abolitionist wing. For a short time, the Republican-led Congress actually used the power of the federal government, against the president's wishes, to protect Black people. The Reconstruction Act of 1867, passed over Johnson's veto, established federal military control of the former Confederate states (except for Tennessee). To be readmitted to the union, they would have to write new constitutions guaranteeing the right to vote and they would have to ratify the Fourteenth Amendment.[26] Thus, the period known as "Radical Reconstruction" began, unleashing, after 250 years of racialized slavery, an experiment in biracial democracy in the South.

Typical of the hypocrisy on matters of race and racism, northern politicians did not pursue the struggle for Black people's freedom and equality with the same zeal in their own backyards. While militarizing the South and forcing southerners to enfranchise Black voters, northern politicians made no such imposition on their own states. Conceding to the unpopularity of Black suffrage among white people nationwide, the Republican Party adopted the stance that whether to grant Black people voting rights in the North should be decided separately by each northern state.[27] Eighty years later, when they dismantled southern Jim Crow, white liberal politicians would likewise craft a legal loophole to allow its northern form to continue undisturbed.[28]

Still, the record of achievements of Black people and their allies in building the infrastructure of public education for all in the US South is a story everyone should know. The Black history curriculum bans today, which at the time of writing are proliferating nationwide, mean that students in those states will have less opportunity to learn about the dramatic educational revolution and counterrevolution that precedes today's conflicts. At the high point of Reconstruction, all over the former Confederacy, new legislatures, with hundreds of Black people participating, wrote and passed new state constitutions establishing free public schools; Texas and South Carolina went further, making attendance compulsory.[29] Among the stories about Florida history that Florida students today may never hear is the one about a Black man, Jonathan Gibbs, who, after serving as secretary of state for three years, was appointed superintendent of public instruction in 1872, overseeing more than 300 schools and 18,000 students of all races.[30] Texas, another flash point in the current book- and curriculum-banning trend, had even more schools: 1,500 by 1872, thanks to Black people and the Republican Party. Student enrollment in Mississippi, Florida, and South Carolina reached approximately half of all children by 1875.[31]

Did Black and white children attend school together in these schools? Mostly, no. But in some places, remarkably, they did. "No state actually required separate schools," historian Eric Foner wrote, "but only Louisiana and South Carolina explicitly forbade them."[32] But "in every state," he added, "blacks objected to constitutional language *requiring* racial segregation."[33] Anecdotes of integrated schooling in the late-nineteenth-century US South show a different future made possible by the revolution of Reconstruction. *The Tribune* of Charleston, South Carolina, wrote, overoptimistically, of the opening of public schools in March of 1865 to all students, regardless of race:

> So the thing is done. The loyal white people—the Irish and German population, have shown that they are quite willing to let their children attend the same school with the loyal blacks; although it is true, that no attempt to unite them in the same room or classes have been tolerated at the time. But in the playgrounds, white and black boys joined in the same sports as they do in the public streets; and there can be no doubt that now that this great

step has been made, all the prejudice against equal educational advantages will speedily vanish.[34]

In Louisiana, a state with a unique history linked to African and Caribbean cultures and rebellions, Republican activists actually tried to create an integrated school system.[35] Louisiana's 1868 constitution was "arguably Reconstruction's most radical document," historian Walter Stern argues, because it proclaimed that everyone would have equal access to schools and other public accommodations "without distinction of race, color or previous condition."[36] The desegregation of New Orleans schools "made them the nation's closest approximations of the common school ideal." Stern wrote,

> For a brief moment, these schools were *public* not simply because taxpayers funded them but because they were places where all members of the community came together. The same could not be said of New York, Baltimore, Philadelphia, or Cincinnati, all of which maintained segregated schools during the 1870s. Indeed, with one-third of its schools racially mixed, New Orleans may very well have had the most integrated system in the country.[37]

Black people took pride in the growing ranks of Black educators (in South Carolina their numbers climbed from fifty in 1869 to more than one thousand in 1875) and in controlling and defining their own institutions, while simultaneously working to abolish color codes from law and public life.[38] "At their most utopian," Foner noted, "blacks in Reconstruction envisioned a society purged of all racial distinctions." Robert

Fitzgerald, a Black teacher, recorded in his diary that he heard a white man talking about how "today is the black man's day" but "tomorrow will be the white man's." Fitzgerald wrote, "I thought, poor man, those days of distinction between colors is about over in this (now) free country."[39]

Tragically, it was not to be so. In hindsight we know what came next: overthrowing democracy and instituting a new system of undemocracy, Jim Crow. Schools were a frequent target for counterrevolutionary violence, as were Black teachers. Reading Robert Fitzgerald's thoughts, we can catch sight of a future that was possible but wasn't allowed to come to pass. As Du Bois put it, "The slave went free; stood a brief moment in the sun; then moved back again toward slavery."[40]

* * *

Thinking about the so-called "redemption" of the US South as a counterrevolution is helpful for explaining the violence, terrorism, and murder to which the white people bent on undoing the progress of Reconstruction resorted. The orgy of post-Reconstruction violence wasn't an irrational outburst of hatred; it was political terrorism. The Ku Klux Klan operated, effectively, as the vigilante arm of the Democratic Party, and its activities included political assassinations.[41] Terrorists assaulted 10 percent of all the Black people elected as delegates to statewide constitutional conventions in 1867–1868 and assassinated six of them.[42] The South was no stranger to lynching as a gruesome tool of social control. But, tellingly, most people lynched in the United States before the Civil War were white, not Black. After the Civil War, the reverse was true.[43]

The ability of the Klan and other armed white supremacist vigilantes to kill with impunity tracked with the will of white northern elites to stop them. When they wanted to curb the violence, they did. In 1870, for instance, President Ulysses Grant created the US Department of Justice to respond to lawlessness in the US South.[44] In that same year, a Republican state government came to power in Texas and oversaw the arrest of four thousand white men in an attempt to halt the violence.[45] In fact, the Klan was successfully suppressed in 1871–1872 by federal marshals who prosecuted their members under the Enforcement Acts.[46] But when Grant and other northern politicians decided they had done enough for Black people and that it was time for the country to "heal," the killings resumed, and the killers were not only not punished but, shamefully, were often welcomed back into the nation's formal political systems. In September 1874 a paramilitary group tried (unsuccessfully) to overthrow the Louisiana state government.[47] A few decades later, one of the participants, former Confederate soldier Edward White, joined the US Supreme Court, becoming its chief justice in 1910.[48]

What changed? In short, the Republican Party (its aging radical wing excepted) abandoned the project of defending Black people's rights in the South because they believed that it was no longer in their interest to do so. For a brief moment, Black people's interests had converged with those of white northern elites. To suppress the slave owners' rebellion, they needed Black people to fight. Later, to help them consolidate their victory over the Confederacy, they needed Black men to vote. But for northern industrialists and politicians, waging a decades-long battle against armed white supremacists and in defense of Black people and their allies in the US South began to contradict their priority of building industrial capitalism in the New South.

Black people in the South were trying to create a more egalitarian society, including a robust social democratic state. In addition to their educational agenda, the freedpeople expected to receive land as a form of reparations. Equitable distribution of productive lands to laboring people was precisely the wrong kind of precedent northern elites wanted to set. Once the Confederacy's rebellion was crushed, they expected the production of cotton to resume and the freedpeople to get back to work producing it at scale. For Republican leaders on the eve of the Gilded Age, the ideals of their abolitionist colleagues seemed outdated, and land reform, which would have been necessary to put the freedpeople on solid financial footing, was simply too radical.[49] Thus, in the ensuing struggle between landowners and the landless, between planters and workers, Black people (the majority of whom were landless workers) were abandoned by their former allies.[50]

Over the next several decades, Black people lost much in that struggle, but not everything. In the infamous compromise of 1877, a devastating setback, the federal government decided to withdraw its troops from the US South. Without the armed support of the federal government, the so-called

Redeemers went on the offensive. But they did so on a political terrain not entirely of their choosing. Black people could still vote, and their power could not be erased overnight. The Redeemers were able to keep schooling underdeveloped, but could not destroy it entirely.[51]

That Black educational institutions survived the counterrevolution is a testament to how quickly Black people had succeeded in establishing them after the war. Schools for Black people were a frequent target of the terrorists: more than 630 were set ablaze in just ten years, from 1866 to 1876.[52] "The sight of blacks carrying books often had the same effect on whites as the sight of armed blacks," historian Leon Litwack wrote, "and many would have found no real distinction between the two threats."[53] In New Orleans, where people of color fought to undermine racial categories in public schooling, white people, in an effort to prevent integrated education, sought to reinforce them. Whereas before, people of unclear ancestry might attend a predominantly white school where officials agreed to "look the other way," now counterrevolutionary white hoodlums stormed through schools, ejecting students who were Black or even whom they suspected of being Black.[54]

In the face of such violent terrorism, Senator Henry Blair proposed one of the last gasps of what Hilary Green calls "educational reconstruction"—legislation to provide federal funding for education, basically to nationalize the "Negro idea" of free public education for all. Blair proposed $77 million for public schools, to be distributed to states over eight years, and according to rates of illiteracy. Three times in the 1880s it came up for a vote and was nearly but never actually passed.[55] Elite northern opinion was against it. "Such government intervention exacerbated northern white fears," Green wrote, "that a labor underclass would 'use government to redistribute wealth.'"[56] Even *The Nation* magazine opposed the bill, ridiculing the need for ongoing federal action. "It is absurd to say that the South in 1888 needs federal aid to educate their children because in 1880 there were three million grown-up illiterates," an editorial sneered, "born either slaves or 'poor whites' of the slavery era."[57] Black education advocates, on the other hand, were confident that the bill would pass and stunned when it didn't.[58]

As has happened so often since, a "post-racial" consensus emerged in the aftermath of Reconstruction among white elites, who converged on the idea that the real problem was not that the idealism of Reconstruction wasn't achieved, but that it had gone too far in the first place. Comparing Reconstruction to the Haitian Revolution and other Black-led insurrections in the Caribbean, Nathaniel Shaler, a Harvard scientist, concluded in the 1880s that "every experiment in freeing the blacks on this continent has in the end resulted in even worse conditions than slavery brought them."[59] The nation's wounds were to be healed, the deep divide reconciled, and the nation's business would be able to resume, by sacrificing the agenda of the people who had just saved the nation—Black people—and elevating the people who had just betrayed it—the former Confederates.

Black educational institutions survived, but the revolutionary tradition of education for liberation lost ground to a new, counterrevolutionary educational ideal: industrial education.

Union Army veteran Samuel Armstrong, a white man, building on his experience with colonial education in Hawaii, founded Hampton Institute in Virginia on the idea that Reconstruction had been a mistake and that Black people needed to focus on "practical" skills and forgo the fight for political and social equality. One of Armstrong's Black students, Booker T. Washington, founded the Tuskegee Institute in the same mold and built a powerful political machine to spread this new educational model as a "solution" to the US "race relations" problem.[60] The rise of Booker T. Washington, the shift of philanthropic support toward industrial education, combined with the defeat of the Blair bill, historian Hilary Green concludes, "ultimately closed the door on the revolutionary moment in African American education."[61]

We would do well to remember the dreams that were nurtured in Reconstruction, and the democratic possibilities that Black people and their allies very nearly realized. Half a century later, the leading lights of the US civil rights movement often referred to their work as a "Second Reconstruction," understanding well that they were building on this legacy.[62] Given the centrality of education to Black people's activism, it's not surprising that the new twentieth-century Black-led movement focused so much on the same thing its nineteenth-century ancestors had. The civil rights movement and its success, represented in popular memory by the *Brown v. Board of Education* decision, unfortunately did not go far enough. Segregation was legally abolished, but in the South the process of desegregation was controlled by white people who largely did not share the movement's broader vision; in the North desegregation was mostly never tried. Once again Black people's activism created a moment of democratic possibility, and once again, powerful white people conspired to thwart their high hopes. When a group of young people in Harlem typed out their agenda for change in 1966, they were picking up the torch.

* * *

In the twenty-first century, US schools are profoundly segregated and unequal, and the legacy of the twentieth-century campaign for desegregation is complicated, to say the least. For starters, northern white politicians made sure that, after the *Brown* decision, "desegregation" would be defined in the 1964 Civil Rights Act (Title IV, Section 401b) in a way that applied to southern schools but not northern ones.[63] Southern school systems were forced to desegregate, but decision-making about how to do so was largely left to white politicians and education leaders, who never consulted Black people about how to do it and assumed that Black educators and Black students and historically Black schools were, by definition, inferior.[64] Thus, despite the fact that the *Brown* decision was a forceful blow to Jim Crow, many Black communities did not experience desegregation as an improvement.

It's true that historically Black schools in the segregated US South were systematically underfunded, but that narrative misses the extent to which Black people were, despite lack of governmental support, nonetheless able to create centers of educational excellence. Ironically, Black educators seeking advanced degrees could not by law attend graduate schools in the South, and yet some were able to seek and gain admission to northern elite graduate schools. Many aspiring Black educators studied there and returned to the South to teach, better educated on average than their white counterparts.[65] All over the US, there were Black high schools that were staffed by brilliant, highly educated Black teachers and principals and had exemplary records of student achievement to show for it. All-Black Sumner High School in Kansas City, Kansas, in the 1940s had several Black teachers with master's degrees, and by the 1950s, some with PhDs, while at neighboring white-only schools, notes education scholar Leslie Fenwick, "teachers rarely had more than a bachelor's degree."[66]

In a remarkable book about the song "Lift Every Voice" (widely known as the Black national anthem), scholar Imani Perry examines the role this song by James Weldon Johnson played in the rich associational life of segregated, closely knit Black communities and especially in their schools in the twentieth century. "Let us march on," the first stanza concludes hopefully, "till victory is won." Among the benefits of growing up in the South, Willam Gray (former president of the United Negro College Fund) remembered, "was that each day in school, we slowly and majestically sang this melodious anthem that was created by one of our poets—a song that promises us that if we keep struggling, we will see the light of freedom because of our faith."[67]

Award-winning historian Annette Gordon-Reed grew up in a segregated Black community in Conroe, Texas. She attended an all-Black school (named for Booker T. Washington) that was staffed with Black educators and, like many of her generation, remembers the experience fondly. "The move toward integration may have killed off one bad thing—Jim Crow education, which would never have truly provided equal funding for two separate educational systems in the town" she wrote,

> but it took some valuable things with it. The notion of "separate" being inherently unequal didn't take account of what it meant for Black students to have Black teachers, particularly at that precise moment in history. Strong bonds existed between teachers and students at Booker T. They were neighbors, relatives (in some cases), and fellow church members. The bonds forged in the classrooms were solidified outside the school, suffusing every aspect of the lives of students and teachers. The "classroom" was everywhere, really.[68]

These historically Black educational institutions emphasized civic education (Black students in segregated Black schools frequently read and studied the US Constitution in its entirety), and, when necessary to avoid the watchful eyes of white leaders, carried on with "fugitive pedagogy" that nonetheless prepared students to join the battle for democracy.[69] The Black church has been widely acknowledged as an essential resource and home base for the US civil rights movement, but new research has begun to highlight the role of historically Black colleges and high schools in nurturing movement ideas and leaders.[70] Even Tuskegee Institute, founded at the apex of the counterrevolution, could by the middle of the twentieth century be aptly described, as one former student did, as a "haven for activist people."[71]

While fighting to overthrow Jim Crow, Black leaders understood that, in the hands of white politicians and education leaders, desegregation threatened to be a disaster for cherished historically Black primary and secondary schools. Dr. Martin Luther King Jr. spoke forcefully to this in 1967, addressing the all-Black Georgia Teachers and Education Association. "Integration doesn't mean the liquidation of everything started and developed by Negroes," he said. "Now there are too many Americans," King continued, "whites and Negroes, who think of integration merely in aesthetic and romantic terms, where you just add a little color to a still predominantly white-controlled power structure. We must see integration in political terms where there is shared power. And I am not one that will integrate myself out of power."[72]

Fully intending to share power in the process, Black educators drew up plans for transferring Black faculty and students to predominantly white schools, and in turn, accepting white students into their institutions. But the white politicians and education leaders in charge had no intention of listening to Black parents, students, or educators. There was nothing about *Brown* or subsequent Supreme Court decisions that required districts to close historically Black schools or to fire Black principals or teachers en masse. But that is precisely what they did. On the assumption that white teachers were superior, that historically white schools were superior, and that Black educators and schools were, by definition, inferior, "integration" came to mean Black students going to predominantly white schools and having white teachers, and almost never the reverse. "The most devastating insult was that in nearly every case," Leslie Fenwick writes, "Black educators who were forced out of school systems were more academically credentialed and professionally experienced than the Whites who replaced them in newly desegregated schools."[73] After years of protest the Senate finally held hearings in 1971 on the mass dismissals of Black educators, but by then it was too late. The numbers available at the time of the hearings revealed a Black educational catastrophe: between 1954 and 1972 nearly half of the nation's Black educators—31,584 Black teachers and 2,235 Black principals—lost their positions in the process of so-called "integration."[74]

Left to the mercy of white educators who mostly viewed them through a deficit lens, Black students were placed in schools where their inferiority was assumed, their culture and history denied, and the adults who cared for them most were unwelcome. In 1969, one newly desegregated school system went to the trouble of discarding new "multiethnic textbooks" they had purchased because "[w]hite parents threatened to burn them."[75] In these hostile environments, Black students often had to stand up for themselves—and they did. But white leaders increasingly responded to Black students' protest actions by criminalizing them. Starting with John F. Kennedy signing new federal "juvenile delinquency" legislation in 1961, several states followed suit, and the emphasis on "law and order" made schools part of the carceral state.[76] If Black students in Black schools with Black educators had been the powerful combination that set the twentieth century on fire, the reaction to desegregation was an attack on all three.[77] Black educators were fired, Black schools were shuttered, and Black students were criminalized.

* * *

Telling the history this way doesn't fully capture the importance of Black teachers, though, or the cost of their absence. "Black children, like Black adults," Fenwick writes, "are required daily to negotiate social, economic, and political structures that engage them first (and sometimes, always) as Black. In these transactions, 'Black' is operationalized by the White-controlled power structure as a deficit and danger. But the presence of Black teachers can stand in opposition to the notion of Black as a deficit."[78] Having a Black teacher supports all students in gaining new perspectives on Blackness and gives Black students resources for challenging racism. To be clear, from what I have observed in my professional career, Black teachers are just as brilliant and just as flawed as any other teachers. But because of the historic destruction of the Black teaching force, and because of the insidious omnipresence of having to negotiate one's Blackness, having a Black teacher can make a difference. That is why, when I see T-shirts that read "Everyone deserves a Black teacher," I tend to agree.[79]

* * *

In New York City, the pattern was different. Black teachers were not fired en masse in New York City after the *Brown* decision, because, for the most part, they were never hired in the first place. New York officially prohibited segregation in public education in 1883, while pioneering the development of subtler systems (such as housing policies, school zoning, admissions policies, school governance, and more) that accomplished the same result.[80] Bureaucratic hurdles likewise prevented Black applicants from being hired as teachers, without any reference to their race. Under the guise of "meritocracy," candidates for teaching had to pass arbitrary tests that rewarded the memorization of obscure trivia and that, through oral exams, punished speakers with southern accents and other nondesirable speech patterns.[81] Meritocracy for some, as historian Christina Collins put it, was institutional racism for others.[82] By the time of the *Brown* decision, New York City had the nation's largest Black population (750,000 people, or 9 percent of the total population).[83] A survey conducted in 1951 found that only 1.5 percent of the city's teachers were Black, and that 91 percent of them taught in "predominantly Negro schools."[84] By 1969, a third of the city's students were Black, but only 9 percent of its teachers were.[85]

Black families moving to New York from the US South were optimistic that their lives in the North would be better. What they found was that segregation was a national problem, as Dr. King described it, "not merely a sectional one."[86] Gotham's leaders spoke boldly against Jim Crow down South but consistently denied that they were presiding over anything similar. White NYC parents' thousands-strong "taxpayer" protests pushed back against desegregation and avoided the real issue, framing their actions as only against "busing"—not against integration.[87] Black residents were unpersuaded; they had decades of experience with northern racism. Twenty years before *Brown*, Ella Baker organized with Harlem parents to challenge the inequalities of New York's school system. Black women like Mae Mallory, whose family migrated from Georgia when she was a child, joined with other Harlem parents in defying mandatory attendance laws by boycotting the schools and naming the school system as segregated. Mallory told a superintendent that her daughter's school was "just as 'Jim Crow' as . . . [those] . . . in Macon, Georgia."[88] In light of Black people's long-standing activism for educational justice in New York, it's not surprising at all that young radicals launched the Black Panther Party in Harlem by focusing on fighting for justice in education.

Their letter is now also part of a collection of items featured on a website designed to help educators and students learn about the intertwined histories of racial and disability justice struggles in New York City schools. Unfortunately, this history remains all too relevant. At the time of writing, a report on New York City Schools confirmed that some 70 percent of them are "intensely segregated."[89] The New York City Civil Rights History Project contains unique historical documents, images, videos, timelines, and contextual information to support the reader in the process of engaging with primary sources. The first impulse that led to the creation of this project came from a dialogue between teen activists and historian Jeanne Theoharis (who later pulled in a large community of collaborators, myself included), grappling with how to understand the history of the phenomenon that they were trying to change: segregated schooling.[90]

On a recent summer day, I shared that 1966 Harlem Black Panther Party letter with a group of teenagers visiting the library. We talked about the fact that the letter proposed to focus the new party's energy on education in Harlem, and we discussed the demands for more Black principals and Black history in the curriculum. As our time together wrapped up, I asked them to reflect on the fact that the authors of the letter were about their age. "They must have been really passionate about this," one student commented. Indeed. In the long view, their passion is not surprising but is part of a long-standing pattern of Black activists equating learning with liberation. Their vision of Black Power in Harlem was not unlike that of their forebears in the US South for whom power meant democracy (not the white supremacists' projection of "Negro domination"). The fact that they had to demand Black principals and Black-themed curricula was the result of destruction of both in too many Black communities after the *Brown* decision, when New York City–style segregation became the template for the nation.[91]

Needless to say, the nation has never even contemplated paying reparations for the history described in this chapter— the burning of Black schools, systematically underfunding Black education, firing Black educators, or overpolicing Black students. In her latest book, education scholar Bettina Love estimates that the educational debt owed to Black students from just the last forty years of anti-Black policies to be $1.5 to $2 trillion in collective lifetime earnings.[92] The total loss going back to the violent overthrow of Reconstruction would be even greater.

Rather than viewing *Brown* as the high-water mark of the struggle for racial justice in education, we need to take a fresh look at Reconstruction, or, as W. E. B. Du Bois called it, Black Reconstruction. Education scholars, Love foremost among them, have explored connections between the nineteenth century movement for abolition and the twenty-first century struggle for educational justice.[93] More broadly, a new generation of activists has taken up the mantle of abolition and call themselves abolitionists, dreaming once again of sweeping social changes to improve our lives.[94] If Black history is any guide, our educational institutions, at all levels, will be crucial battlegrounds of, and resources for, the mightier work of reconstruction.

Back to the Library

JAMES BALDWIN, ONE OF THE most important literary and political figures of the twentieth century represents, to me, another way in which Black history is for everyone. Although he was deeply rooted in and wrote and spoke from the specific vantage of point of the Afro-American experience, Baldwin repeatedly emphasized that the significance of that experience was global. "You think your pain and your heartbreak are unprecedented in the history of the world," he famously said. "But then you read. It was books that taught me that the things that tormented me the most were the very things that connected me with all the people who were alive, who had ever been alive."[1]

Baldwin returned to a variation on that theme in Florida in 1963, addressing an audience of educators. In that speech, published a few months later as "A Talk to Teachers," he mused about the possibility that engaging with Black history truthfully might be liberatory for non-Black students:

> It is not really a "Negro revolution" that is upsetting the country. What is upsetting the country is a sense of its own

identity. If, for example, one managed to change the curriculum in all the schools so that Negroes learned more about themselves and their real contributions to this culture, you would be liberating not only Negroes, you'd be liberating white people who know nothing about their own history. And the reason is that if you are compelled to lie about one aspect of anybody's history, you must lie about it all. If you have to lie about my real role here, if you have to pretend that I hoed all that cotton just because I loved you, then you have done something to yourself.[2]

If by lying we have, as Baldwin suggests, done something to ourselves, then by studying Black history and getting closer to the truth(s) of our shared past, we have a chance to liberate ourselves.

That James Baldwin developed these ideas and was able to communicate them so forcefully in novels and essays and interviews read and viewed around the world was surely due to his immense intellectual abilities. But he also, from an early age, had access to caring adults in two important institutions that nurtured his gifts: public schools and public libraries. James Baldwin wasn't born into wealth or privilege, but he had, in 1930s Harlem, spaces for transformation. His elementary school principal at PS 24, Gertrude Ayer, the first Black woman appointed to that rank in New York City, remembered him as having a "haunted look"; Ayer assigned a white intern, Orisha "Bill" Miller, to work with him.[3] Bill Miller took her young charge to movies and theatrical productions all over the city (including an all-Black production of Macbeth, directed

by Orson Welles, set in revolutionary Haiti!) and had a profound, lifelong impact on him.[4] At Frederick Douglass Middle
School, the famed Harlem Renaissance poet Countee Cullen
was his French teacher and likely planted the idea for Baldwin's later sojourn to Paris. His middle school's literary journal
had a Harvard-trained math teacher, Herman Porter (coinci-
dentally also known as "Bill"), also a Black man, as its faculty
advisor. He assigned young James, the journal's editor, to write
about Harlem's history and personally intervened to give him a
life-changing experience with research to develop it.

Bill Porter picked up his promising pupil from his home
(ignoring James Baldwin's father's disapproval) and escorted
him to the main research library on Fifth Avenue, downtown.
Together, they passed between the famous lions and walked
up the marble stairs. Later, in his first novel, *Go Tell It on the
Mountain*, James's narrator would pass by the building and
dream of going inside.[5] Bill Porter introduced James to some
of the librarians, got him started on his research, and gave him
enough cash to take a taxi back home.[6]

Learning this story recently, and seeing its echoes in his ma-
ture work, I thought: James Baldwin's teachers brought him
to the library and changed his life. The resulting essay from
that first assignment ("Harlem—Then and Now"), a series of
vignettes depicting everyday Harlem life in selected moments
over several centuries and beginning in 1636, Porter thought,
was "superb."[7] Other teachers encouraged him to visit the
135th Street Library (known today as the Schomburg Center)
where he claims to have "read everything." On his deathbed,

James Baldwin stated that he wanted his personal papers to be kept there; and they are.[8]

The really transformative possibility, as Baldwin identified, would be for young people to read as widely as he did, and in doing so, discover, as he did, a feeling of connection to the pain of others. The possibility that, as a result, all young people might grow up questioning white supremacy and national chauvinism (not to mention heteropatriarchy) is surely the real motivation for the proliferating book and curriculum bans throughout the United States at the time of writing. Such censorship is nothing new to Black teachers. Now, educators nationwide who want to teach Black history can turn to Black history themselves to learn the grassroots strategies of resistance, fugitive pedagogy, and community building that Black people and Black educators have cultivated throughout the twentieth century. The work of Arturo Schomburg, Carter G. Woodson, Mary Mcleod Bethune, Ella Baker, and Septima Clark are now essential resources, not only for students, but for all educators who find themselves working, educating, and trying to thrive in repressive conditions.[9]

These bans are not the first contemporary attempts, though, to limit the curriculum more broadly in public schools. We are still reckoning with the disastrous effects of the shift, several decades long, to high-stakes standardized testing as the raison d'être of schooling. Presumably a policy intended to protect the most vulnerable and underserved students, its practical impact was to narrow the curriculum to that which could be measured on a standardized exam.[10] I know this from bitter experience.

In my very first year as a teacher in a public school in Harlem, I cut out large bright blue letters spelling the phrase "IF THERE IS NO STRUGGLE, THERE IS NO PROGRESS" and carefully taped them to the wall, near the ceiling, at the front of my classroom. It was a quote from a speech Frederick Douglass gave about the impossibility of reform without conflict.[11] My students and I returned to those words many times throughout the year, discussing their various possible meanings. I also tried to encourage my students to see them as a mantra for the learning process. My students were extremely bright, and many of them were exceptionally quick-witted and funny. At first, teaching seemed easy because our conversations were so lively and intelligent. But then, as required, I administered a practice test for the state exam, and they bombed it. I was shocked. This was not a "gifted" class, but I knew my students and was convinced of their gifts. As I worked through their errors and tried to help them correct each one, my suspicion grew that such tests were of limited value. I wanted for them the kind of project-based learning with intrinsically interesting material that I was privileged to have had, not just staring day after day at decontextualized text excerpts and the questions someone else thought to ask about them. As my teacher, Ms. Brooks, had done, I reached for the Black Arts movement and its writers and I reached for Black history and its most inspiring stories of resistance to give my students a feeling that they were building on a powerful legacy. I tried my best to counteract the implicit judgment of the standardized tests and encourage my students to keep struggling. I wish I had taken them to the library.

* * *

In early December 2021, on a cool, crisp day, I made my way to a school on the Upper East Side to be one of several guest speakers in a daylong program broadly organized on the theme of education as a human right. My presentation was going to be on the long struggle for Black studies. I prepared notes on the history of fugitive literacy efforts during enslavement, about the compulsory ignorance laws, the dual legacy of segregated schooling, and the explosive twentieth-century high school and college struggles for Black studies. But when I finally got to my assigned classroom, only six students showed up. I was disappointed that there were no visibly Black students present, but the small audience also presented an opportunity to hear more from the attendees. So I scrapped my presentation and instead asked each student to speak about why they had come. "I don't know that much on this topic," one young man said. "Given our world today, and worldwide events, I thought it would be good to learn more," another young man near him said. "I want to expand my knowledge," said another. These three were on one side of the room (to my left). On the other side of the room, two young women and a young man, I came to realize, constituted an entirely different camp. They were self-identified antiracist activists who had come to speak with me to gain intellectual resources for that work.

I spoke briefly about some of what I had learned from reading and studying Black history, and as I asked more questions of the students, the perspectives of the young men to my left became clear. They were, they confessed one at a time, deeply concerned about the idea that kindergarten students were being taught critical race theory (CRT). I asked how they knew this was the case, and they said this was something they had heard on the news. I gently disagreed that that was true, but thanked them for raising these ideas, and encouraged them to say more. They did. All of the right-wing talking points poured forth one by one: CRT is teaching white kids that they are inherently racist; these ideas are being foisted on kids at inappropriate ages; and the real goal of this instruction is to undermine faith in the United States of America as a political project. "They hate America," one young man said, "and they don't know how much worse it is other places."

I had encountered this kind of thinking my whole life. So many of my classmates growing up were steeped in it. Eddie Glaude describes it as a "sense of self rooted in liberty, self-reliance, and hard work" that "validates who white Americans take themselves to be . . . and the specialness of America itself."[12] But as a young person, I didn't have the vocabulary to argue back; I didn't know different stories to tell or ways to validate or even learn more about my instinctive disagreement. I didn't have Black history. And now, here I was again encountering the same mindset, except I was the adult and the authority (to some extent) in the room, having spent years in pursuit of this knowledge. Yet, even with this knowledge, I have learned how important it is to listen at least as much as I speak. I know that all of the privileges of my new social position make it easy to miss my blind spots, so I try to remember that I never know (unless they tell me) my interlocutor's own pain or history.

That day, I took a breath, and patiently explained that CRT was created by legal scholars; it is something that is taught in law school and sometimes in other higher education classrooms, not in elementary school.[13] I am always willing to try to help young people think through their assumptions and invite them to consider another view: in this case, that Black history is not a threat to white students, but it is a threat to white supremacy. My young allies in the room chimed in, speaking about how learning Black history had opened their eyes. They shared a story about a music teacher who had helped them see (and hear) the profound influence of Black music on all US music genres. Acknowledging the long history of Black patriotism seemed like another way to build a bridge to the doubters in the room, so I spoke about the way Black people had consistently played a leading role in advocating for freedom and democracy—the very ideals the nation espoused as central to its self-identity. But the young men to my left were unmoved. And our time was running out.

I took advantage of the opportunity to have the last word by leaving them with a few questions: What if learning Black history didn't lead you to believe in racial categories, but to question them? What if Black history showed that the loyalty Black people offered the United States was rarely granted to them in return? What if believing in the inherent superiority of the United States made it harder to learn about the world and our place in it? As they left the room, each student in turn shook my hand and thanked me for the conversation.

"They hate America." These young men have been led to believe that Black history is problematic because it is fundamentally unpatriotic. Little do they know that so many of the leading lights of Black-led social movements in North America did, in fact, fight for change from a place of love, including love of country. But it won't do to respond, "No, everyone you learn about when you study Black history loved America" or "Black history is American history." That's not true, either, and it's really beside the point. Nations of people, like races of people, are relatively new in human history, and therefore it is entirely appropriate that we consider them both as objects of study, including critical study, not unquestioned loyalty. Classrooms are places for critical inquiry, debate, and disagreement. Emotions are part of the learning process, and teaching is relational. As a guest speaker, I didn't know anything about those young men, their stories or their motivations, and they knew very little about me. We didn't have to agree. We could view the same evidence and come to different conclusions. In classrooms across the country, though, something more is possible. In the process of a deeper engagement with Black history, teachers and students are also learning about each other.

* * *

After the most recent presidential election, a surge of liberal commentators quickly concluded that "wokeness" had gone too far.[14] According to this line of thinking, all the progressive thinking on gender, race, and sexuality had alienated young people like those I encountered as a guest speaker. I was taken aback, but I shouldn't have been surprised. It hurts to see progress on the chopping block, but that just makes Black history more urgent and necessary. Once again, as we've seen so many times in the past, after a brief moment of hope and forward movement, it feels as though Black people—and other vulnerable populations—are to be sacrificed at the national altar. Once again the nation is to be reconciled, the angry young men appeased, but at the expense of the modest efforts made to accommodate a broader spectrum of humanity in workplaces, classrooms, media, bookshelves, and curricula.

I would argue, however, that the problem is not actually that "wokeness" went too far, but that it didn't go far enough. The roots of antiracism have always been in bottom-up movements that dream of changing everything and making life better for everyone. Against the zero-sum thinking that has become dominant in the present, the Black feminists who coined the concept of "identity politics" (which itself has been attacked by the same people who criticize critical race theory) argued that if Black women were free, everyone would be free.[15] But stripped of this broader redistributive agenda, antiracism has become prey to what Olúfẹ́mi O. Táíwò and others have dubbed "elite capture"—diluted to a set of slogans made safe for corporate emails and lawn signs, and limited in its ability to win hearts and minds.[16] A new way of talking and thinking is cold comfort if it's not part of creating a better way of living.

It's not easy to keep an open mind, especially when we feel like our ideas (and our lives) are under attack. Librarians, teachers, students, and parents have to defend our public institutions, defend the right to read freely, and, at the same time, stay curious ourselves. In a recent research methods course, I told my students that if, after investigating something closely and gathering new evidence, you end up thinking exactly what you thought starting out, you're probably doing it wrong. Learning is about struggling with new information and ideas, and it doesn't always feel good to revise what you thought you knew. We have to leave room, in our classrooms, in our movements, and in our lives, for questions, even heretical ones, because, as Nikole Hannah-Jones has argued, our search for truth and understanding has no natural limit. Against those who would narrow our reading lists, or tell us which questions are acceptable to ask, we need political and intellectual horizons that are as wide as possible.[17]

Black history continues to surprise me, and I wrote this book to share the ways that my own ongoing reading and teaching has forced me to revise my thinking about the categories of race and nation. It has shown me that the Haitian Revolution overturned the racist foundations of the modern world—and remains a source of inspiration for people dreaming of social change more than two hundred years later. And I continue to be astounded by the transformative ambitions of Radical Reconstruction, as I learn more stories from that revolutionary era. With full knowledge of their complications and shortcomings, the paths not taken and visions only partially realized,

Black people can take pride in such moments of daring action and radical dreaming. But they are not for Black people alone. These dreams often transgress and transcend racial and national boundaries. They are a gift to all of us, if we are willing to receive them. With all of our flaws, with all of our limitations, and with our eyes wide open, we must continue to read, write, and dream. Black history is for everyone.

Acknowledgments

I've been working on this book, one way or another, for about ten years. In addition to activist spaces and study groups (if you know, you know), so much of what I've learned has been through dialogue with students, at many different levels. I'm grateful to my elementary students at PS 125 and PS 30 in Harlem and PS 261 in Brooklyn, my high school students in the College Now program at Baruch College and in the Voices of a People's History program, my graduate students in the Hunter College School of Education, and my doctoral students in the PhD Program in Urban Education at the City University of New York Graduate Center. Before this book was written, it was spoken in countless talks, panels, and seminars, building on ideas I developed in my first book. I'm grateful to have had the opportunity to work through these concepts while guest lecturing in high school classrooms at the invitations of teachers, including Lev Moscow, Becca Zimmerman, and Bill Linville, with undergraduate and graduate students at the invitations of Naomi Murakawa, Robbie Cohen, Keeanga-Yamahtta Taylor, Erik Wallenberg, Anderson Bean, Natalia Ortiz and Christian Siener, Marjorie Feld, Deborah Gray, Rhonda Collier, Bettina Love, and Phillip Smith.

I'm also grateful for opportunities to address multiple groups of educators gathered by the Folger Shakespeare Library at the invitation of Peggy O'Brien, with educators organized through the Black and Latino Employee Networking and Development group in NYC Public Schools, in the Philadelphia School District's Africana Studies Seminar organized by Ismael Jimenez, and with educators nationwide through the Zinn Education Project. Thanks to LaNitra Berger for the invitation to share my perspectives with students and faculty in the annual W. E. B. Du Bois Lecture at George Mason University and to Tracie D. Hall and Marieke Van de Laar for the wonderful opportunity to speak with students, faculty, and special guests in the Freedom Summit at the University College Roosevelt. I tried out ideas in workshop form that contributed to the first and fourth chapters on Star Island at the invitation of Bernadette Clemens—thank you. And thank you also to Mark Stern for bringing your students to the library and challenging me to share a draft excerpt of this book with them.

I discuss several of my education projects in this book, and there are more colleagues who worked on them than I can acknowledge, but I want to offer special thanks to continuous support and encouragement from my Schomburg Center colleagues, including Joy Bivins, Kevin Matthews, Tammy Lawson, Maira Liriano, Brent Edwards, M. Scott Johnson, Virginia Dixon, and Cara Hill. Thanks to Kevin Young for taking a chance on me. Barrye Brown, Charlie Carter, Novella Ford, and Jafari Sinclair Allen gave me the precious opportunity to participate in commemorations of James Baldwin's centennial year, which pushed me to read and learn more about the influence of teachers and librarians on his trajectory. I am so grateful to Nikole Hannah-Jones, Kimberlé Crenshaw, Bettina Love, and Khalil Muhammad for the chance to learn from you in public dialogues at the Schomburg Center. Mariame Kaba and Adam Sanchez pushed my thinking about Black Reconstruction in a series of workshops coproduced by Novella Ford. Thanks to my National Endowment for the Humanities summer institute colleagues, especially Ansley Erickson, Matt Kautz, Khadijah Akeem, GeColby Youngblood, Karen Taylor, Juan Bencosme, and Subha Ahmed, as well as all of the teachers who traveled to New York City to learn about the history of educational activism in Harlem. I'm proud to have contributed to, and continue to learn from, the Conversations in Black Freedom Studies series, founded by Jeanne Theoharis and Komozi Woodard, and now curated by Jeanne and Robyn Spencer. Thanks always to two of my greatest teachers, Howard Zinn and Jean Anyon.

Nicole Daniels and Lauren O'Brien did the lion's share of research and writing for the Schomburg Curriculum Project, which is finally seeing the light of day thanks to additional support from the Center for Educators and Schools and particularly its curriculum department led by Alex Tronolone. That project had a top-notch advisory board: Adam Sanchez, Yolanda Sealey-Ruiz, Ansley Erickson, and Jesse Hagopian. Arturo Agüero's decision to include a session on the Haitian Revolution in the New York Public Library's 2023 Educator Summer Residency was fortuitous, and Vanessa Valdés is always an inspiration; her lecture and suggested reading list transformed the third chapter. I continue to learn so much from Tiffany James, Liz Billy, and all of my NYPL colleagues. Special thanks to Dan Landsman whose good counsel keeps me grounded, to my colleagues in Communications who sharpen my thinking, and to Brian Bannon, Brent Reidy, and Tony Marx whose encouragement keeps me writing. The NYC Civil Rights History Project team is too large to list, but kudos to the stellar leadership of Ansley Erickson, Jeanne Theoharis, and Jessica Murray. I'm so proud of the small but mighty Voices of a People's History team, bringing history to life in schools and stages nationwide: Anthony Arnove, Martha Redbone, David Johnson, Matthew Covey, Jordana Leigh, Anna Strout, and Shade Adeyemo. Through Voices, I've also learned so much from recent programs featuring Akemi Kochiyama, Haley Pessin, Zakiya Collier, Imani Perry, and Eddie Glaude. I continue to be inspired by the visionary Tuskegee community members who are lifting up the important histories of the town and the campus, including (but not limited to!) Norma Jackson, Lucenia Dunn, George Paris, and Guy Trammel. Special thanks to Sandy and Harvey Taylor for making my latest visit there extra special.

Years ago Bhaskar Sunkara and John Mulholland invited me to contribute to *Jacobin* and *The Guardian*, respectively, and those two pieces formed the basis of the first chapter—thank you. People who were generously willing to read early drafts of these chapters, or patiently endured hearing me talk about them, or just offered helpful words of encouragement include Mamyrah Prosper, Dominique Jean-Louis, Robert Robinson, Matt Gonzalez, Robbie Cohen, Steve Brier, Brendan Kiely, Sadye Campoamor, Lamson Lam, Eric Baudelaire, Julie Golia, Helen Warwick, Michael Pourfar, Filip Stabrowski, Sherry Deckman, Zachary Price, Chris Myers, Brenda Coughlin, Joe Rogers, Bill Kelly, Buzz and Ursula Tenny, Ron Livingston, Jeremy McCarter, and Juvanie Piquant—thank you. I'm grateful for the Soccer Community of Inwood and my no-guilt book club—they keep me healthy in body, mind, and spirit in all seasons. Youna Kwak and Munro Galloway helped me get away to write and were generous listeners and hosts. Crucial conversations with my comrades Róisín Davis (also my agent) and Anthony Arnove shaped the earliest versions of this book. Julie Fain and the whole team at Haymarket Books are outstanding, but I am especially grateful to Katy O'Donnell; your editorial comments, judgment, queries, and provocations were superb. Jon Key's cover design is just stunning. Thank you.

My mother and father, whose family histories are traced in the first chapter, gave essential support to this project, as well as extremely helpful comments and feedback. My cousin Tammy Brown shared research on the Crawley side, greatly expediting my research process. I'm so grateful for my brother Rick and his family, Jacquie, Ryan, and Patrick; my stepmother Cenellia; and my family by marriage, Mohamad, Jen, Michael, Alex, and Caroline. My children, Nina and Omar, understood when I needed to get out of the apartment in the early mornings, evenings, and weekends in which this book was mostly written. They've been curious about its contents and enjoyed gently teasing me about the due date(s). My wife, Susie, helps me lead with curiosity in all things. What can I say? You were right all along.

Notes

Epigraph

Quoted in Karen Thorsen, director, *James Baldwin: The Price of the Ticket*, American Masters (PBS), August 14, 1989, season 4, episode 4. The 135th Street Library is today known as the Schomburg Center for Research in Black Culture, one of the research libraries of the New York Public Library. In addition to viewing free exhibitions, anyone can walk in without an appointment, go down to the Jean Blackwell Hutson Research and Reference Division on the lower level, ask for books, and sit down to read them. All you need is a library card, and if you don't have one, the librarians will give you one.

Introduction

1 See, for example Gholdy Muhammad's second book, *Unearthing Joy: A Guide to Culturally and Historically Responsive Teaching and Learning* (New York: Scholastic, 2023).

2 An act relating to individual freedom, SB 148, the Florida Senate, 2022, https://www.flsenate.gov/Session/Bill/2022/148/.

3 Robin D. G. Kelley, "The Long War on Black Studies," *New York Review of Books*, June 17, 2023, https://www.nybooks.com/online/2023/06/17/the-long-war-on-black-studies/.

4 Isabel Wilkerson, *Caste: The Origins of Our Discontents* (New York: Random House, 2020), 15–16.

5 Barack Obama, "Remarks by the President at Black History Month Reception," February 18, 2016, https://obamawhitehouse.archives.gov/the-press-office/2016/02/18/remarks-president-black-history-month-reception.

6 David Boaz, "Black History Is American History," *Cato Institute*, February 11, 2015.

7 Brian Jones, "Washington and Canada: Free Market Idealism in the Context of Social Defeat," *Journal of Negro Education*, 86, no. 1 (2018): 33–45.

8 Heather McGhee, *The Sum of Us: What Racism Costs Everyone and How We Can Prosper Together* (New York: One World, 2021).

9 See Ana Rosado, Gideon Cohn-Postar, and Mimi Eisen, *Erasing the Freedom Struggle: How State Standards Fail to Teach the Truth About Reconstruction*, Zinn Education Project, 2022, https://www. teachreconstructionreport.org.

10 "Freedom Dreams: Juneteenth-Inspired Professional Learning for NYC Educators," Center for Educators and Schools, June 9, 2022, Schomburg Center for Research in Black Culture, New York Public Library, https://www.youtube.com/live/ TBtzeWdmHcw?si=d0NtXE8m6gaCBmkm.

11 *Teaching Hard History: American Slavery*, Southern Poverty Law Center, 2018, https://www.splcenter.org/wp-content/uploads/files/ tt_hard_history_american_slavery.pdf; Rosado et al., *Erasing the Freedom Struggle*.

12 My recent reading list has included Herman L. Bennett, *African Kings and Black Slaves: Sovereignty and Dispossession in the Early Modern Atlantic* (Philadelphia: University of Pennsylvania Press, 2018); Howard W. French, *Born in Blackness: Africa, Africans, and the Making of the Modern World, 1471 to the Second World War* (New York: Liveright, 2021); Cheikh Anta Diop, *Precolonial Black Africa* (Chicago: Lawrence Hill Books, 1987); Christopher Ehret, *Ancient Africa: A Global History, to 300 CE* (Princeton: Princeton University Press, 2024); Chester Higgins, *Sacred Nile* (New York: March Forth Imprint, 2021); Zeinab Badawi, *An African History of Africa: From the Dawn of Humanity to Independence* (New York: Mariner Books, 2024).

1. Race

1 This chapter incorporates material from two previously published articles: "The Social Construction of Race," *Jacobin*, June 25, 2015, and "Growing Up Black in America: Here's My Story of Everyday Racism," *Guardian*, June 6, 2018.

2 1st Congress, 2nd Session (March 26, 1790), *Congressional Record*, 103–4.

3   163 US 537 (1896).

4   *Corpus Juris*, quoted in Cheryl I. Harris, "Whiteness as Property,"
     Harvard Law Review 106, no. 8 (June 1993): 1707–91.

5   In fairness, my older brother Rick, a defense attorney, had probably
     tried to prepare me for this sort of thing.

6   W. E. B. DuBois, *The Souls of Black Folk* (1903; New York: Oxford,
     2007), 8.

7   Carol C. Mukhopadhyay, et al., *How Real Is Race? A Sourcebook on
     Race, Culture, and Biology*, 2nd ed. (New York: Alta Mira, 2013),
     53–54.

8   Mukhopadhyay, et al., *How Real Is Race?* 75.

9   I acknowledge that many reasonable people see this differently and
     have evidence to support their view. There clearly were ways of
     categorizing people and putting them into hierarchies that precede and
     certainly formed the basis for our modern conception of race. Ibram
     X. Kendi convincingly traces the origins of anti-Black ideas in *Stamped
     from the Beginning: The Definitive History of Racist Ideas in America*
     (New York: Nation Books, 2016), and in *Black Marxism: The Making
     of the Black Radical Tradition* (1983; Chapel Hill: University of North
     Carolina Press, 2000), Cedric J. Robinson emphasizes the continuity
     between these earlier patterns and the form that emerged under
     capitalism. In this chapter, I emphasize the rupture—the new ways
     that anti-Black ideas became institutionalized.

10   Barbara Jeanne Fields, "Slavery, Race and Ideology in the United
     States of America," *New Left Review* 181, no. 1 (1990), 102.

11   Robin Blackburn, *The American Crucible: Slavery, Emancipation and
     Human Rights* (London: Verso, 2011), 109.

12   Edmund S. Morgan, *American Slavery, American Freedom: The Ordeal
     of Colonial Virginia* (New York: Norton, 1975), 324.

13   Ira Berlin, *Many Thousands Gone: The First Two Centuries of Slavery in
     North America* (Cambridge: Harvard University Press, 1998).

14   Berlin, *Many Thousands Gone*, 29–30.

15   Morgan, *American Slavery*, 299.

16   William Waller Hening, ed., *The Statutes at Large; Being a Collection
     of All the Laws of Virginia, from the First Session of the Legislature, in the
     Year 1619*, vol. 2 (New York, 1823).

17   Morgan, *American Slavery*, 250–69.

18 Quoted in Theodore W. Allen, *The Invention of the White Race, Vol. II: The Origin of Racial Oppression in Anglo-America* (1997; New York: Verso, 2012), 241.

19 Berlin, *Many Thousands Gone*, 44–45.

20 Berlin, *Many Thousands Gone*, 124.

21 The genealogical information I gathered came from three main sources: a family history written by my father, Robert F. Jones, *The Lawrence Weaver and Wiley Jones Families*, 2nd ed. (2008; Twinsburg: Self-Published, 2013); another written by a cousin on my mother's side, Marion Golightly Crawford, *Crawley Family Reunion: 1989* (Detroit: self-published, 1989); and using names and information from these two, I conducted further research on Ancestry.com.

22 Jones, *Weaver and Jones Families*.

23 Eugene W. Milteer Jr., *North Carolina's Free People of Color: 1715–1885* (Baton Rouge: LSU Press, 2020).

24 Jones, *Weaver and Jones Families*, 37.

25 It's interesting to note the ways that Blackness is defined differently outside of the United States. *Black* has been a term of political identification for people of Asian as well as African origin in the United Kingdom. See, for example, Anandi Ramamurthy, "The Politics of Britain's Asian Youth Movements," *Race & Class* 48, no. 2 (2006): 38–60.

26 Barbara J. Fields and Karen E. Fields, *Racecraft: The Soul of Inequality in American Life* (New York: Verso, 2012), 109.

27 Edwidge Danticat, *We Are Alone: Essays* (Minneapolis: Graywolf Press, 2024), 76.

28 Ruth Wilson Gilmore, "Fatal Couplings of Power and Difference: Notes on Racism and Geography," *Professional Geographer* 54, 1 (2002), 16.

2. Nation

1 David W. Blight describes the occasion in a remarkable biography, *Frederick Douglass: Prophet of Freedom* (New York: Simon & Schuster, 2018), 229–36. Cheryl A. Wall discusses Douglass's literary and rhetorical work in this speech in *On Freedom and the Will to Adorn: The Art of the African American Essay* (Greensboro: University of North Carolina Press, 2018), 67–75.

2   The full text of the speech is available in John Stauffer and Henry
     Louis Gates Jr., eds., *The Portable Frederick Douglass* (New York:
     Penguin Books, 2016), 195–222.

3   For more information on this organization, see www.peopleshistory.us.

4   My performance version is excerpted from an excerpt of the speech in
     Howard Zinn and Anthony Arnove, *Voices of a People's History of the
     United States, 10th Anniversary Edition* (New York: Seven Stories Press,
     2009), 183–86.

5   Seven Stories Press Presents Readings from *Voices of a People's History
     of the United States*, NY Society for Ethical Culture, 2004, https://
     www.youtube.com/watch?v=PD3hYsAB698.

6   LaGarrett J. King, "Black History Is Not American History: Toward
     a Framework of Black Historical Consciousness," *Social Education* 84,
     no. 6 (2020): 335–41.

7   Martha S. Jones, *Birthright Citizens: A History of Race and Rights in
     Antebellum America* (New York: Cambridge University Press, 2018).

8   W. E. B. DuBois, *Black Reconstruction in America: Toward a History
     of the Part Which Black Folk Played in the Attempt to Reconstruct
     Democracy in America, 1860–1880* (1936; New York: Atheneum, 1969).

9   Paul Le Blanc and Michael Yates, *A Freedom Budget for All Americans:
     Recapturing the Promise of the Civil Rights Movement in the Struggle for
     Economic Justice Today* (New York: Monthly Review Press, 2013).

10   Brian Jones, "Keys to the Schoolhouse: Black Teachers, Education
     Reform and the Growing Teacher Rebellion," in *What's Race Got to
     Do with It? How Current School Reform Policy Maintains Racial and
     Economic Inequality*, 2nd ed., eds. Edwin Mayorga, Ujju Aggarwal,
     and Bree Picower (New York: Peter Lang, 2020), 63–86.

11   David Cooper and Julia Wolfe, "Cuts to the State and Local Public
     Sector Will Disproportionately Harm Women and Black Workers,"
     Economic Policy Institute, July 9, 2020, https://www.epi.org/blog/
     cuts-to-the-state-and-local-public-sector-will-disproportionately-harm-
     women-and-black-workers/.

12   Ana Lucia Araujo, *Reparations for Slavery and the Slave Trade: A
     Transnational and Comparative History* (London: Bloomsbury, 2017).
     This history is one of many reasons I argue that this demand deserves
     our attention in the twenty-first century; see Brian Jones, "The
     Socialist Case for Reparations," in *Reparations and Reparatory Justice:
     Past, Present, and Future*, eds. Sundiata Keita Cha-Jua, Mary Frances

Berry, and V. P. Franklin (Urbana: University of Illinois Press, 2024), 178–88.

13 Beverly Gage, "What an Uncensored Letter to M.L.K. Reveals," *New York Times Magazine*, November 11, 2014.

14 Sam Levin, "FBI Terrorism Unit Says 'Black Identity Extremists' Pose a Violent Threat," *Guardian*, October 7, 2017.

15 C. Vann Woodward, *The Strange Career of Jim Crow* (New York: Oxford University Press, 1955), 70.

16 Quoted in Blight, *Frederick Douglass*, 737.

17 Edmund Morgan, *American Slavery, American Freedom: The Ordeal of Colonial Virginia* (New York: Norton, 1975).

18 Sean Wilentz, *The Rise of American Democracy: Jefferson to Lincoln* (New York: Norton, 2005), 118.

19 Annette Gordon-Reed and Peter Onuf, *"Most Blessed of the Patriarchs": Thomas Jefferson and the Empire of the Imagination* (New York: Liveright, 2016).

20 Eric Foner, "The Significance of Reconstruction in American History," 2013 James A. Field Lecture in History, October 28, 2013, Swarthmore College, New York, https://www.swarthmore.edu/news-events/eric-foner-significance-reconstruction-american-history.

21 Keisha Blain writes about how Fannie Lou Hamer often spoke of the promise—and limitations—of the US Constitution in *Until I Am Free: Fannie Lou Hamer's Enduring Message to America* (Boston: Beacon Press, 2021).

22 Sylvia Frey, "The American Revolution and the Creation of a Global African World," in *From Toussaint to Tupac: Black Internationalism Since the Age of Revolution*, eds. Michael O. West, William G. Martin, and Fanon Che Wilkins (Chapel Hill: University of North Carolina Press, 2009); Ashley D. Farmer, *Remaking Black Power: How Black Women Transformed an Era* (Chapel Hill: University of North Carolina Press, 2017), 129.

23 Garrett Felber, *Those Who Know Don't Say: The Nation of Islam, the Black Freedom Movement, and the Carceral State* (Chapel Hill: University of North Carolina Press Books, 2019).

24 Les Payne and Tamara Payne, *The Dead Are Arising: The Life of Malcolm X* (New York: Liveright, 2020); Manning Marable, *Malcolm X: A Life of Reinvention* (New York: Penguin, 2011).

25 Malcolm X, "The Ballot or the Bullet" (April 3, 1964), speech delivered in Cleveland, Ohio (and again on April 12 in Detroit,

Michigan), https://americanradioworks.publicradio.org/features/blackspeech/mx.html.

26 Malcolm X, "Message to the Grass Roots" (November 10, 1963), speech delivered in Detroit, Michigan, at the Northern Grass Roots Leadership Conference, in George Breitman, ed., *Malcolm X Speaks: Selected Speeches and Statements* (New York: Grove Weidenfeld, 1990).

27 Marable, *Malcolm X*, 124.

28 Payne, *Dead Are Arising*, 439.

29 Payne, *Dead Are Arising*, 443.

30 Payne, *Dead Are Arising*, 446–47.

31 Payne, *Dead Are Arising*, 446–47.

32 Marable, *Malcolm X*, 252–53; Payne, *Dead Are Arising*, 448.

33 David Helps, "'We Charge Genocide': Revisiting Black Radicals' Appeals to the World Community," *Radical Americas 3*, no. 9 (2018): 2–24.

34 Helps, "'We Charge Genocide,'" 4–5.

35 Helps, "'We Charge Genocide,'" 7, 11.

36 Civil Rights Congress, *We Charge Genocide: The Historic Petition to the United Nations for Relief from a Crime of the United States Government against the Negro People* (New York: Civil Rights Congress, 1951).

37 Helps, "'We Charge Genocide,'" 13. The founding statement of Malcolm's secular organization, the Organization of Afro-American Unity, read, in part: "[We are p]ersuaded that the Charter of the United Nations, the Universal Declaration of Human Rights, the Constitution of the United States and the Bill of Rights are the principles in which we believe and that these documents if put into practice represent the essence of mankind's hopes and good intentions."

38 Marable, *Malcolm X*; Peniel E. Joseph, *The Sword and the Shield: The Revolutionary Lives of Malcolm X and Martin Luther King Jr.* (New York: Basic Books, 2020).

39 Joseph, *Sword and Shield*, 449.

40 Quoted in Marable, *Malcolm X*, 272.

41 Dan Berger, "SNCC's Unruly Internationalism," *Boston Review*, November 16, 2021.

42 Quoted in Blain, *Until I Am Free*, 96.

43 Quoted in Michael Eric Dyson, *I May Not Get There with You: The True Martin Luther King, Jr.* (New York: Free Press, 2000), 55.

44 Blain, *Until I Am Free*, 103.

45 Brian Jones, *The Tuskegee Student Uprising: A History* (New York: NYU Press, 2022), 107–8.

46 Clayborne Carson, *In Struggle: SNCC and the Black Awakening of the 1960s* (Cambridge: Harvard University Press, 1981), 189.

47 Berger, "SNCC's Unruly Internationalism."

48 Robyn Spencer, "Merely One Link in the Worldwide Revolution: Internationalism, State Repression, and the Black Panther Party," in *From Toussaint to Tupac*, 217.

49 Spencer, "Merely One Link," 219.

50 Spencer, "Merely One Link," 220.

51 Spencer, "Merely One Link," 221.

52 "J. Edgar Hoover: Black Panther Greatest Threat to U.S. Security," *United Press International*, July 16, 1969, https://www.upi.com/Archives/1969/07/16/J-Edgar-Hoover-Black-Panther-Greatest-Threat-to-US-Security/1571551977068/.

53 Russell Rickford, *We Are an African People: Independent Education, Black Power, and the Radical Imagination* (New York: Oxford University Press, 2016), 132.

54 Rickford, *We Are an African People*, 154; Farmer, *Remaking Black Power*, 120.

55 Quoted in Farmer, *Remaking Black Power*, 135.

56 Farmer, *Remaking Black Power*, 134–37.

57 Rickford, *We Are an African People*, 157.

58 Quoted in Rickford, *We Are an African People*, 160.

59 Kwame Ture and Charles Hamilton, *Black Power: Politics of Liberation in America* (New York: Vintage, 1967).

60 Franz Fanon, *The Wretched of the Earth*, transl. Constance Farrington (New York: Grove, 1963).

61 Africa Information Service, ed., *Return to the Source: Selected Speeches by Amilcar Cabral* (New York: Monthly Review Press, 1973), 78.

62 Ta-Nehisi Coates notes the resonance between Zionism and Black nationalism, for example, and "shudders" to imagine what would be lost if the latter had been as successful as the former, in *The Message* (New York: One World, 2024), 209–10, and symmetry with Black Americans' colonization of Liberia, 159; see also the complicated consequences of Haitian nation-building described in chapter four.

63 Barbara J. Fields, "Eugene D. Genovese," *Georgia Historical Quarterly* 98/4 (2014): 345–49. Fields continued, wryly, "As [fellow historian

Eric] Hobsbawm pointed out, there is no such thing as global government or a global citizen. In fact, the globe is not a political entity at all, but an abstraction as remote as any other astronomical object—which, when you think about it, is what the globe is."

64 Quoted in Millery Polyné, *From Douglass to Duvalier: US African Americans, Haiti, and Pan Americanism, 1870–1964* (Gainseville: University Press of Florida, 2010), 38.

65 Leslie M. Alexander, *Fear of a Black Republic: Haiti and the Birth of Black Internationalism in the United States* (Urbana: University of Illinois Press, 2023), chapter 7.

66 Quoted in Polyné, *From Douglass to Duvalier*, 29.

67 Polyné, *From Douglass to Duvalier*, 28.

68 Polyné, *From Douglass to Duvalier*, 49.

69 Brandon R. Byrd, *The Black Republic: African Americans and the Fate of Haiti* (Philadelphia: University of Pennsylvania Press, 2020), 109.

70 Quoted in Byrd, *The Black Republic*, 107.

71 Byrd, *The Black Republic*, 111; Polyné, *From Douglass to Duvalier*, 45.

72 Quoted in Polyné, *From Douglass to Duvalier*, 50; see also Byrd, *The Black Republic*, 116.

73 Quoted in Blight, *Frederick Douglass*, 705.

74 Byrd, *The Black Republic*, 116.

75 Blight, *Frederick Douglass*, 706.

76 Blight, *Frederick Douglass*, 702.

77 Blight, *Frederick Douglass*, 705.

78 Byrd, *Black Republic*, 118.

79 Blight, *Frederick Douglass*, 710.

80 Quoted in Polyné, *From Douglass to Duvalier*, 53.

3. Revolution

1 Schomburg Center for Research in Black Culture, Manuscripts, Archives and Rare Books Division, The New York Public Library. "Resolution of the Savannah City Council to prevent Black people from entering the city following the Haitian Revolution." New York Public Library Digital Collections. Accessed March 4, 2025. https://digitalcollections.nypl.org/items/510d47db-c1ae-a3d9-e040-e00a18064a99.

2   Teaching with the Schomburg Center's Archives, made possible by
    a grant from the Institute for Museum and Library Services, is now
    available online: https://www.schomburgcenter.org/curriculum.
    "Abolition as a Black-Led Movement," Teaching with the Schomburg
    Center's Archives, https://www.nypl.org/spotlight/center-for-educators/
    primary-sources/schomburg-abolition-black-led-movement.

3   Manisha Sinha, *The Slave's Cause: A History of Abolition* (New Haven:
    Yale University Press, 2016).

4   Leslie M. Alexander, *Fear of a Black Republic: Haiti and the Birth
    of Black Internationalism in the United States* (Urbana: University of
    Illinois Press, 2023).

5   Quoted in Alexander, *Fear of a Black Republic*, 31.

6   Leon A. Waters, "Jan. 8, 1811: Louisiana's Heroic Slave Revolt,"
    ZinnEdProject.org, https://www.zinnedproject.org/news/tdih/
    louisianas-slave-revolt/.

7   Howard W. French, *Born in Blackness: Africa, Africans, and the Making
    of the Modern World, 1471 to the Second World War* (New York:
    Liveright, 2021), 333.

8   Quoted in Alexander, *Fear of a Black Republic*, 39.

9   Laurent Dubois makes this argument in *Avengers of the New World:
    The Story of the Haitian Revolution* (Cambridge: Harvard University
    Press, 2004).

10 Jeremy Popkin discusses some of these complications in a 2021 review
    of the literature, "The Haitian Revolution Comes of Age: Ten Years of
    New Research," *Slavery & Abolition*, 42, 2 (2021): 382–401.

11 Catherine Porter, Constant Méheut, Matt Apuzzo, and Selam
    Gebrekidan, "The Root of Haiti's Misery: Reparations to
    Enslavers," *New York Times*, May 20, 2022, https://www.nytimes.
    com/2022/05/20/world/americas/haiti-history-colonized-france.html.

12 French, *Born in Blackness*, 353.

13 C. L. R. James, *The Black Jacobins: Toussaint L'Ouverture and the San
    Domingo Revolution*, 2nd ed., revised (1963; New York: Vintage, 1969),
    55.

14 French, *Born in Blackness*, 357.

15 Timothy M. Matthewson, "George Washington's Policy," *Diplomatic
    History* 3, no. 3 (July 1979): 327; Julius S. Scott, *The Common Wind:
    Afro-American Currents in the Age of the Haitian Revolution* (2018;
    London: Verso, 2020), 55.

16 James, *Black Jacobins*, 55.

17 Porter, et al., "Root of Haiti's Misery."

18 Quoted in Jean Casimir, *The Haitians: A Decolonial History* (University of North Carolina, 2020), 72.

19 Dubois, *Avengers*, 40.

20 Dubois, *Avengers*, 41.

21 John Thornton, "I Am a Subject of the King of Congo: African Political Ideology and the Haitian Revolution," *Journal of World History* 4, no. 2 (1993): 185.

22 Thornton, "I Am a Subject," 201.

23 Thornton, "I Am a Subject," 108–9.

24 Thornton, "I Am a Subject," 186.

25 Casimir, *The Haitians*, 350.

26 Casimir, *The Haitians*, 349.

27 Casimir, *The Haitians*, 288.

28 Casimir, *The Haitians*, 293–94.

29 David Geggus, "Marronage, Voodoo, and the Saint Domingue Slave Revolt of 1791," *Proceedings of the Meeting of the French Colonial Historical Society* 15 (1992): 22–35.

30 Casimir, *The Haitians*, 293–94.

31 The summer educator residency program is produced by NYPL's Center for Educators and Schools and supported, in its first three years, by the Whiting Foundation. See https://www.nypl.org/spotlight/educators-summer-residency. The theme in 2023 was "Histories of the Future," https://www.nypl.org/blog/2023/04/27/histories-future-summer-residency-center-educators-and-schools; Vanessa K. Valdés is the author of several books, including *Diasporic Blackness: The Life and Times of Arturo Alfonso Schomburg* (Albany: SUNY Press, 2017).

32 Toussaint L'Ouverture, "Proclamation," August 29, 1793, quoted from Jean-Bertrand Aristide, *Toussaint L'Ouverture: The Haitian Revolution* (2008; London: Verso, 2019), 1–2.

33 Dubois, *Avengers*, 178.

34 Haitian Constitution of 1801, quoted from Aristide, *Toussaint L'Ouverture*, 46.

35 Quoted in James, *The Black Jacobins*, 334 and in Dubois, *Avengers*, 278.

36 Casimir, *The Haitians*, 59.

37 Quoted in Marlene L. Daut, "Beyond Trouillot: Unsettling Genealogies of Historical Thought," *small axe* 25, no. 1, 64, (2021): 144.

38 Casimir, *The Haitians*, 150.

39 Dubois, *Avengers*, 188–93.

40 Dubois, *Avengers*, 192.

41 Dubois, *Avengers*, 235–39.

42 Dubois, *Avengers*, 205.

43 Thornton, "I Am a Subject," 199.

44 Quoted in Scott, *Common Wind*, 150.

45 Quoted in French, *Born in Blackness*, 362.

46 Quoted in Gordon-Reed and Onuf, *"Most Blessed of the Patriarchs,"* 283.

47 Quoted in Scott, *Common Wind*, 204–5.

48 Sean Wilentz, *The Rise of American Democracy: Jefferson to Lincoln* (New York: Norton, 2005), 109.

49 Matthewson, "George Washington's Policy," 324, 326.

50 Matthewson, "George Washington's Policy," 328.

51 Quoted in Gerald Horne, *Confronting Black Jacobins: The US, the Haitian Revolution, and the Origins of the Dominican Republic* (New York: Monthly Review Press, 2015), 7.

52 Matthewson, "George Washington's Policy," 327.

53 Matthewson, "George Washington's Policy," 321.

54 Matthewson, "George Washington's Policy," 336.

55 French, *Born in Blackness*, 367.

56 Quoted in French, *Born in Blackness*, 372.

57 French, *Born in Blackness*, 374.

58 The twists and turns of US policy toward revolutionary Haiti are well discussed in Horne, *Confronting Black Jacobins*.

59 Dubois, *Avengers*, 235–39.

60 Marlene L. Daut, "'Alpha and Omega,' of Haitian Literature: Baron de Vastey and the U.S. Audience of Haitian Political Writing," *Comparative Literature* 64, no. 1 (2012): 60.

61 Alexander, *Fear of a Black Republic*, 57.

62 French, *Born in Blackness*, 398.

63 Quoted in French, *Born in Blackness*, 401.

64 Annette Gordon Reed, "We Owe Haiti a Debt We Can't Repay," *New York Times*, July 21, 2021, https://www.nytimes.com/2021/07/21/opinion/haiti-us-history.html.

65 Dubois, *Avengers*, 7.

66 Casimir, *The Haitians*, xix.

67 Dubois, *Avengers*, 129.

68 Michel-Rolph Trouillot, *Silencing the Past: Power and the Production of History* (Boston: Beacon Press, 1995), 88.

69 Casimir, *The Haitians*, "Preface," xii.

70 Casimir, *The Haitians*, 21.

71 Casimir, *The Haitians*, 297.

72 Sven Beckert describes these similar battles to enforce commodity production as a new way of life in *Empire of Cotton: A Global History* (New York: Vintage, 2014).

73 Casimir, *The Haitians*, 142.

74 Casimir, *The Haitians*, 97.

75 Lorenzo Ravano, "The Borders of Citizenship in the Haitian Revolution," *Political Theory* 49, no. 5 (2021): 725.

76 Casimir, *The Haitians*, 393.

77 Aristide, *Toussaint L'Ouverture*, xix.

78 David Geggus, "The Naming of Haiti," *New West Indian Guide* 71, nos. 1–2 (1997): 43.

79 Dubois, *Avengers*, 299.

80 Geggus, "The Naming of Haiti," 58.

81 1805 Haitian Constitution; Dubois, *Avengers*, 300.

82 Dubois, *Avengers*, 294–95.

83 Porter et al., "The Root of Haiti's Misery."

84 Porter et al., "The Root of Haiti's Misery."

85 Lazaro Gamio, Constant Méheut, Catherine Porter, Selam Gebrekidan, Allison McCann and Matt Apuzzo, "The Ransom: Haiti's Lost Billions," *New York Times*, May 20, 2022, https://www.nytimes.com/interactive/2022/05/20/world/americas/enslaved-haiti-debt-timeline.html.

86 Alexander, *Black Republic*, 73.

87 Porter et al., "The Root of Haiti's Misery."

88 Gina Athena Ulysse, *Why Haiti Needs New Narratives: A Post-Quake Chronicle* (Middletown: Wesleyan University Press, 2015), 7.

89 David Brooks, "The Underlying Tragedy," *New York Times*, January 14, 2010, https://www.nytimes.com/2010/01/15/opinion/15brooks.html. Marlene L. Daut discusses implications in "Daring to Be Free /

Dying to Be Free: Towards a Dialogic Haitian-U.S. Studies," *American Quarterly* 63, no. 2 (June 2011): 375–89.

90 Quoted in Popkin, "Haitian Revolution Comes of Age," 396.

91 Frederick Douglass, "Lecture on Haiti," The World's Fair, January 2, 1893.

92 See Daut, "Daring to Be Free," 377, 385.

93 Mamyrah Dougé-Prosper and Mark Schuller, "End of Empire? A View from Haiti," *NACLA Report on the Americas* 53, no. 1 (2021): 1.

94 Dubois, *Avengers*, 89.

95 Quoted in Daut, "Alpha and Omega," 55–56.

96 Trouillot, *Silencing the Past*, 89.

4. Education

1   See Black Panther Party Harlem Branch files, Sc MG 80, Schomburg Center for Research in Black Culture, Manuscripts, Archives and Rare Books Division, The New York Public Library, https://archives.nypl.org/scm/20948.

2   See Suzanne Cope, *Power Hungry: Women of the Black Panther Party and Freedom Summer and Their Fight to Feed a Movement* (Chicago: Chicago Review Press, 2021); Alondra Nelson, *Body and Soul: The Black Panther Party and the Fight Against Medical Discrimination* (Minneapolis: University of Minnesota Press, 2011); Robert P. Robinson, *Stealin' the Meetin': The Roots & Legacy of the Black Panther Party's Oakland Community School* (New York: NYU Press, forthcoming).

3   The Oakland party had a slightly different name, owing to its emphasis on challenging police brutality: The Black Panther Party for Self-Defense.

4   Donna Murch, "When the Panther Travels: Race and the Southern Diaspora in the History of the BPP, 1964–1972," in *Black Power Beyond Borders: The Global Dimensions of the Black Power Movement*, ed. Nico Slate (New York: Palgrave, 2012).

5   Robin D. G. Kelley, *Freedom Dreams: The Black Radical Imagination* (Boston: Beacon Press, 2002), ix.

6   For more information on this institute, Harlem's Education Movements: Changing the Civil Rights Narrative (Schomburg NEH Summer Institute for Teachers), funded by the National Endowment for the Humanities, see https://harlemeducationmovements.com/.

With Ernest Morrell, Ansley T. Erickson coedited the first book-length study on the history of education activism in Harlem: *Educating Harlem: A Century of Schooling and Resistance in a Black Community* (New York: Columbia University Press, 2019), available in an enhanced digital version online: http://book.harlemeducationhistory.org/.

7   I was fortunate to learn more about Yuri Kochiyama's life and legacy at the November 2023 conference "Building Racial Solidarity in Black and Asian American History Across K–20 Education," organized by Judy Yu and Yolanda Sealey-Ruiz at Teachers College, Columbia University.

8   Barbara Ransby, *Ella Baker and the Black Freedom Movement: A Radical Democratic Vision* (Chapel Hill: University of North Carolina Press, 2003), 69–70. Watch "Dr. Ashley Farmer on Mae Mallory," https://www.youtube.com/watch?v=eIhNF5yHplc and "Dr. Paula Marie Seniors on Mae Mallory," https://www.youtube.com/watch?v=CUpY_l0YrBw from Harlem's Education Movements, 2021.

9   On the 1964 boycotts, see the "The 1964 Boycotts," NYC Civil Rights History Project, https://nyccivilrightshistory.org/topics/boycotting-ny-schools/1964-boycotts/.

10 Brian Jones, "The Struggle for Black Education," in *Education and Capitalism: Struggles for Learning and Liberation*, eds. Jeff Bale and Sarah Knopp (Chicago: Haymarket Books, 2012), 41–69.

11 347 U.S. 483 (1954).

12 Kimberlé Crenshaw, Neil Gotanda, Gary Peller, and Kendall Thomas, eds. *Critical Race Theory: The Key Writings That Formed the Movement* (New York: New Press, 1995).

13 Mary L. Dudziak, *Cold War Civil Rights: Race and the Image of American Democracy* (Princeton: Princeton University Press, 2011), 90.

14 Leah N. Gordon, *From Power to Prejudice: The Rise of Racial Individualism in Midcentury America* (Chicago: University of Chicago Press, 2019).

15 Quoted in Eric Foner, *The Second Founding: How the Civil War and Reconstruction Remade the Constitution* (New York: W.W. Norton & Company, 2019), 53.

16 W. E. B. DuBois, *Black Reconstruction in America: Toward a History of the Part Which Black Folk Played in the Attempt to Reconstruct Democracy in America, 1860–1880* (1936; New York: Atheneum, 1969), 185.

17 Heather Andrea Williams, *Self-Taught: African American Education in Slavery and Freedom* (Chapel Hill: University of North Carolina Press, 2009), 7.

18 Jones, "Struggle for Black Education."

19 Herbert George Gutman, "Schools for Freedom: The Post-Emancipation Origins of Afro-American Education," in Gutman and Ira Berlin, eds., *Power & Culture: Essays on the American Working Class* (New York: Pantheon Books, 1987), 260–97.

20 Jones, "Struggle for Black Education."

21 Quoted in DuBois, *Black Reconstruction*, 641–42.

22 James D. Anderson, *The Education of Blacks in the South, 1860–1935* (Chapel Hill: University of North Carolina Press, 1988), 6.

23 Anderson, *Education of Blacks in the South*, 21.

24 Quoted in Anderson, *Education of Blacks in the South*, 22.

25 Eric Foner, *A Short History of Reconstruction, 1863–1877* (New York: Harper Perennial, 1990), 96.

26 Foner, *Second Founding*, 90.

27 Foner, *Second Founding*, 96.

28 Leslie T. Fenwick, *Jim Crow's Pink Slip: The Untold Story of Black Principal and Teacher Leadership* (Cambridge: Harvard Education Press, 2022), 40.

29 Foner, *Short History of Reconstruction*, 138.

30 Du Bois, *Black Reconstruction*, 654–55.

31 Foner, *Short History of Reconstruction*, 157.

32 Foner, *Short History of Reconstruction*, 139.

33 Foner, *Short History of Reconstruction*, 139.

34 Quoted in Du Bois, *Black Reconstruction*, 643.

35 Foner, *Short History of Reconstruction*, 157.

36 Walter C. Stern, *Race and Education in New Orleans: Creating the Segregated City, 1764–1960* (Baton Rouge: Louisiana State University Press, 2018), 42.

37 Stern, *Race and Education in New Orleans*, 44.

38 Foner, *Short History of Reconstruction*, 158.

39 Quoted in Foner, *Short History of Reconstruction*, 127.

40 Du Bois, *Black Reconstruction*, 40.

41 See Jack M. Bloom, *Class, Race, and the Civil Rights Movement* (Bloomington: Indiana University Press, 1987) and Foner, *Short History of Reconstruction*, 146.

42 Manisha Sinha, *The Rise and Fall of the Second American Republic: Reconstruction, 1860–1920* (New York: Liveright, 2024), 190.

43 Eugene D. Genovese, *Roll, Jordan, Roll: The World the Slaves Made* (New York: Vintage, 1976), 33–34.

44 Sinha, *Rise and Fall of the Second American Republic*, 243.

45 Sinha, *Rise and Fall of the Second American Republic*, 246.

46 Foner, *Second Founding*, 121.

47 Stern, *Race and Education in New Orleans*, 44.

48 Foner, *Second Founding*, 130.

49 Foner, *Short History of Reconstruction*, 135; Sinha, *Rise and Fall of the Second American Republic*.

50 "The failure of the victors to expropriate their land as well and distribute it among the freedmen," Barbara J. Fields wrote, "placed the planters at an advantage in the ensuing struggle." See "The Nineteenth Century American South," *Plantation Society*, Vol II, No 1 (April, 1983), 11.

51 Anderson, *Education of Blacks in the South*, 23.

52 Jarvis R. Givens, "Black Education as the General Strike: The Radical Origins of African American Teaching and Learning," *Journal of African American History*, 109, no. 2 (2024): 252.

53 Leon F. Litwack, *Trouble in Mind: Black Southerners in the Age of Jim Crow* (New York: Knopf, 1998), 87.

54 Sian Zelbo, "E. J. Edmunds, School Integration, and White Supremacist Backlash in Reconstruction New Orleans," *History of Education Quarterly*, 59, no 3, 2019.

55 Hilary Green, *Educational Reconstruction: African American Schools in the Urban South, 1865–1890* (New York: Fordham University Press, 2016), 186.

56 Green, *Educational Reconstruction*, 192.

57 Green, *Educational Reconstruction*, 188.

58 Green, *Educational Reconstruction*, 190–91.

59 Quoted in Khalil Gibran Muhammad, *The Condemnation of Blackness: Race, Crime, and the Making of Modern Urban America* (Cambridge: Harvard University Press, 2010), 17.

60 Michael R. West, *The Education of Booker T. Washington: American Democracy and the Idea of Race Relations* (New York: Columbia University Press, 2006). Industrial education essentially attempted to reconcile Black people's educational ambitions with white people's fear that Black people's movements had gone too far. Born in the counterrevolution, "[T]he 'Hampton-Tuskegee idea' represented," historian James Anderson concluded, "the ideological antithesis of the educational and social movement begun by ex-slaves." See Anderson, *Education of Blacks in the South*, 33.

61 Green, *Educational Reconstruction*, 195.

62 See Manning Marable, *Race, Reform, and Rebellion: The Second Reconstruction and Beyond in Black America, 1945–2006* (1984; New York: Bloomsbury, 2018); Keisha N. Blain, *Until I Am Free: Fannie Lou Hamer's Enduring Message to America (Boston: Beacon Press, 2021).*

63 See "Title IV of the Civil Rights Act of 1964, Excerpt," in NYC Civil Rights History Project, https://nyccivilrightshistory.org/gallery/title-iv-civil-rights-act/.

64 Ansley T. Erickson, *Making the Unequal Metropolis: School Desegregation and Its Limits* (Chicago: University of Chicago Press, 2016).

65 Fenwick, *Jim Crow's Pink Slip*, 40.

66 Quoted in Fenwick, *Jim Crow's Pink Slip*, Preface.

67 Quoted in Imani Perry, *May We Forever Stand: A History of the Black National Anthem* (Chapel Hill: University of North Carolina Press, 2018), 88.

68 Annette Gordon-Reed, *On Juneteenth* (New York: W.W. Norton, 2021), 49.

69 Jon N. Hale, *A New Kind of Youth: Historically Black High Schools and Southern Student Activism, 1920–1975* (Chapel Hill: University of North Carolina Press, 2022); R. Givens, *Fugitive Pedagogy: Carter G. Woodson and the Art of Black Teaching* (Cambridge: Harvard University Press, 2021).

70 See Joy Williamson-Lott, *Radicalizing the Ebony Tower: Black Colleges and the Black Freedom Struggle in Mississippi* (New York: Teachers College Press, 2008); Robert Cohen, David J. Snyder, and Dan T. Carter, eds., *Rebellion in Black and White: Southern Student Activism in the 1960s*; Martha Biondi, *The Black Revolution on Campus* (Berkeley: University of California Press, 2012); Jelani M. Favors, *Shelter in a Time of Storm: How Black Colleges Fostered Generations of Leadership*

and Activism (Chapel Hill: University of North Carolina Press, 2019); Jones, *Tuskegee Student Uprising*; Hale, *A New Kind of Youth*.

71 Quoted in Jones, *Tuskegee Student Uprising*, 25.

72 Quoted in Vanessa Siddle Walker, *The Lost Education of Horace Tate: Uncovering the Hidden Heroes Who Fought for Justice in Schools* (New York: New Press, 2018), 7–8. King's attitude toward the process of integration was "a message that America missed," Walker wrote.

73 Fenwick, *Jim Crow's Pink Slip*, 5.

74 Fenwick, *Jim Crow's Pink Slip*, 7.

75 Fenwick, *Jim Crow's Pink Slip*, 52.

76 Hale, *A New Kind of Youth*, 174.

77 Hale, *A New Kind of Youth*, 175.

78 Fenwick, *Jim Crow's Pink Slip*, 142.

79 According to a 2022 study, Black students who have at least one Black teacher by third grade are 13 percent more likely to graduate and 19 percent more likely to enroll in college. See Gershenshon et al., "Long-Run Impacts of Same Race Teachers," *American Economic Journal: Economic Policy*, 14 (4): 300–42.

80 See "How Did NYC Segregate Its Schools?" https://nyccivilrightshistory.org/topics/how-did-nyc-segregate/.

81 Christina Collins, *"Ethnically Qualified": Race, Merit, and the Selection of Urban Teachers, 1920–1980* (New York: Teachers College Press, 2011), 78–80.

82 Collins, *"Ethnically Qualified,"* 5.

83 Matthew F. Delmont, *Why Busing Failed: Race, Media, and the National Resistance to School Desegregation* (Oakland: University of California Press, 2016), 29.

84 Quoted in Collins, *"Ethnically Qualified,"* 109.

85 Collins, *"Ethnically Qualified,"* 122.

86 Quoted in Tahir Butt, "'You Are Running a de Facto Segregated University': Racial Segregation and the City University of New York, 1961–1968," in *The Strange Careers of the Jim Crow North*, eds. Brian Purnell, Jeanne Theoharis, and Komozi Woodard (New York: New York University Press, 2019), 188.

87 See Delmont, *Why Busing Failed*.

88 Quoted in Kristopher Bryan Burrell, "Black Women as Activist Intellectuals: Ella Baker and Mae Mallory Combat Northern Jim

Crow in New York City's Public Schools During the 1950s," in *Strange Careers of the Jim Crow North*, 100.

89 NYC Comptroller, "Intentional and Inclusive School Mergers: Prioritizing Real Integration as NYC Works to Reduce Class Size and Address Declining Enrollment," May 6, 2024, https://comptroller.nyc. gov/reports/intentional-and-inclusive-school-mergers/.

90 See "Project History," NYC Civil Rights History Project, https:// nyccivilrightshistory.org/project-history/.

91 Diana D'Amico Pawlewicz, *Blaming Teachers: Professionalization Policies and the Failure of Reform in American History* (New Brunswick: Rutgers University Press, 2020), 10.

92 Bettina L. Love, *Punished for Dreaming: How School Reform Harms Black Children and How We Heal* (New York: St. Martin's Press, 2023), 280.

93 Bettina L. Love, *We Want to Do More Than Survive: Abolitionist Teaching and the Pursuit of Educational Freedom* (Boston: Beacon Press, 2019). See also "Abolitionist Teaching and the Future of Our Schools," featuring Bettina L. Love, Gholdy Muhammad, Dena Simmons, and Brian Jones. Sponsored by Haymarket Books and the Schomburg Center for Research in Black Culture. June 23, 2020, https://www. youtube.com/watch?v=uJZ3RPJ2rNc.

94 Angela Y. Davis, Gina Dent, Erica R. Meiners, and Beth E. Richie, *Abolition. Feminism. Now.* (Chicago: Haymarket Books, 2022).

Epilogue

1   Quoted in Jane Howard, "Doom and glory of knowing who you are," *LIFE* Volume 54, No 21, May 24, 1963, 89.

2   Quoted in Karen Thorsen, director, *James Baldwin: The Price of the Ticket*, American Masters (PBS), August 14, 1989, season 4, episode 4.

3   Quoted in Herb Boyd, *Baldwin's Harlem: A Biography of James Baldwin* (New York: Atria Books, 2008), 14. Daniel Perlstein explores the work of Gertrude Ayer in the context of the work of other progressive educators in Harlem during 1930s in "Schooling the New Negro: Progressive Education, Black Modernity, and the Long Harlem Renaissance," in *Educating Harlem: A Century of Schooling and Resistance in a Black Community*, eds. Ansley T. Erickson and Ernest Morrell (New York: Columbia University Press, 2019), 31–54.

4   See David Adams Leeming, *James Baldwin: A Biography* (New York: Knopf, 1994), chapter 2. James Baldwin writes about Miller's impact on him in *The Devil Finds Work* (1976; New York: Knopf, 2011), 5–9.

5   James Baldwin, *Go Tell It on the Mountain* (1953; New York: Vintage, 2024), 31.

6   Boyd, *Baldwin's Harlem*, 20–21.

7   Fern Marja Eckman, *The Furious Passage of James Baldwin* (New York: M. Evans and Company, 1966), 51–55.

8   Quoted in Thorsen, *James Baldwin*. See also James Baldwin Papers, Division of Manuscripts and Rare Books, Schomburg Center for Research in Black Culture, The New York Public Library, https://archives.nypl.org/scm/24143.

9   See Vanessa K. Valdés, *Diasporic Blackness: The Life and Times of Arturo Alfonso Schomburg* (Albany: SUNY Press, 2017); R. Givens, *Fugitive Pedagogy: Carter G. Woodson and the Art of Black Teaching* (Cambridge: Harvard University Press, 2021); Noliwe Rooks, *A Passionate Mind in Relentless Pursuit: The Vision of Mary Mcleod Bethune* (New York: Penguin, 2024); Barbara Ransby, *Ella Baker and the Black Freedom Movement: A Radical Democratic Vision* (Chapel Hill: University of North Carolina Press, 2003); Katherine M. Charron, *Freedom's Teacher: The Life of Septima Clark* (Chapel Hill: University of North Carolina Press, 2009); and Jesse Hagopian, *Teach Truth: The Struggle for Antiracist Education* (Chicago: Haymarket Books, 2025). I explored the resonance between this history and the twenty-first century antiracist movement in education in "Black Lives Matter in School: Historical Perspectives," in *Black Lives Matter at School: An Uprising for Educational Justice*, eds. Denisha Jones and Jesse Hagopian (Chicago: Haymarket Books, 2020), 25–32.

10 Brian Jones, "Standardized Testing and Students of Color," in *More Than a Score: The New Uprising Against High-Stakes Testing*, ed. Jesse Hagopian (Haymarket Books, 2014), 71–76.

11 Frederick Douglass, *Two Speeches, by Frederick Douglass; One on West India Emancipation, Delivered at Canandaigua, Aug. 4th, and the Other on the Dred Scott Decision, Delivered in New York, on the Occasion of the Anniversary of the American Abolition Society, May 1857* (Rochester: C.P. Dewey, Printer, 1858), 22, https://babel.hathitrust.org/cgi/pt?id=mdp.69015000003026&seq=24.

12 Eddie S. Glaude Jr., *Begin Again: James Baldwin's America and Its Urgent Lessons for Our Own* (New York: Crown, 2020), 80–81.

13 Victor Ray, *On Critical Race Theory: Why It Matters and Why You Should Care* (New York: Random House, 2022).

14 Maureen Dowd, "Democrats and the Case of Mistaken Identity Politics," *New York Times*, November 9, 2024. https://www.nytimes.com/2024/11/09/opinion/democrats-identity-politics.html.

15 Keeanga-Yamahtta Taylor, "Until Black Women Are Free, None of Us Will Be Free," *New Yorker*, July 20, 2020, https://www.newyorker.com/news/our-columnists/until-black-women-are-free-none-of-us-will-be-free.

16 Olúfẹ́mi O. Táíwò, *Elite Capture: How the Powerful Took Over Identity Politics (and Everything Else)* (Chicago: Haymarket Books, 2022).

17 Atasi Das, Robert Robinson, Brian Jones, and Edwin Mayorga with Jordan Bell and Karen Zaino, "Keep That Horizon as Broad as Possible: A Community Conversation on Abolitionist Praxis in Education," *Theory, Research, and Action in Urban Education* 9, no. 1 (Fall 2024), https://traue.commons.gc.cuny.edu/keep-that-horizon-as-broad-as-possible-a-community-conversation-on-abolitionist-praxis-in-education/.

Index

"Passim" (literally "scattered") indicates intermittent discussion of a topic over a cluster of pages.

abolitionism, 49, 82–83, 104, 121, 125, 131, 144, 182n93
Africa, human origins in, 23
African history, 13
African postcolonial leaders, 64–65, 70
Africans
    in Atlantic colonies, 25–29
    in colonial Virginia, 29–35 passim
    in the Haitian Revolution, 85–91
Alexander, Leslie, 83
American Revolution, 8–9, 102, 110, 111
Anderson, James, 124, 179–80n60
Anderson, Sam, 117
anticommunism, 63, 65, 73
antiracism, 154
Aristide, Jean Bertrand, 104
Armstrong, Samuel, 134
arson of schools, 132
assimilation, 19
The Autobiography of Malcolm X, 2
Ayer, Gertrude, 146

Bacon, Nathaniel, 32, 35
Bacon's Rebellion, 31–32, 35
Baker, Ella, 118, 142, 148

Baldwin, James, 145–48
"The Ballot or the Bullet" (Malcolm X), 58–59
Bandung Conference, 1955, 60
Belafonte, Harry, 65–66
Berger, Dan, 65, 68
Berkeley, William, 32
Berlin, Ira, 29
Black Arts Movement, 20, 117, 149
The Black Jacobins (James), 87, 88, 92, 93
Black Lives Matter, 42
Black nationalism, 170n62
Blackness, 17, 21, 42–44 passim
    Haiti, 105, 109
Black Panther Party (Alabama), 114
Black Panther Party (BPP), 64, 65, 68–69, 73, 115
    Kathleen Cleaver, 71
    New York City, 116
Black Panther Party (Harlem), 113–18, 142, 143
Black Power: The Politics of Liberation in America (Ture and Hamilton), 71–72
Black studies, 150
Black teachers, 19, 124, 129, 136–41, 147–48
Blair, Henry, 132–33

185

Blight, David, 77, 78
Bonaparte, Napoleon. *See* Napoleon
    I, emperor of the French
boycotts, 118, 142
Boyer, Jean-Pierre, 107
Britain: Haiti and, 94, 98
Brooks, David, 108
Brown v. Board of Education, 10,
    119–21, 134, 135, 138, 144
Bureau of Refugees, Freedmen, and
    Abandoned Lands. *See* Freedmen's
    Bureau

Cabral, Amílcar, 72
Carmichael, Stokely. *See* Ture,
    Kwame
Casimir, Jean: *The Haitians: A
    Decolonial History*, 89, 92–93, 103,
    104, 106
Center for Educators and Schools, 3,
    164n10, 173n31
Chase, Frank, 124
citizenship, 16, 49
    Haiti, 104
Civil Rights Act of 1964, 135
civil rights movement, 8, 118, 134,
    137. *See also* King, Martin Luther,
    Jr.
Civil War, 50, 53, 75, 110, 122, 123,
    130–31
Cleaver, Kathleen, 71
Clyde, William, 77, 79
Coates, Ta-Nehisi, 170n62
Cold War, 64, 121
Collins, Christina, 141
colonial settlers, 26–35 passim
commodity production and
    consumption, 27–28, 31
complexion. *See* skin color
Constitution, US. *See* US
    Constitution
critical race theory (CRT), 151, 154

Cullen, Countee, 147

Daniels, Nicole, 82
Danticat, Edwidge, 41–42
Democratic Party, 58, 65
    Reconstruction, 129
desegregation, 10, 120, 133–42
    passim, 138, 139
    New Orleans schools, 128
Dessalines, Jean-Jacques, 96, 97
Dominican Republic, 75
Dougé-Prosper, Mamyrah, 110
Douglass, Frederick, 45–48, 52–56
    passim, 121, 149
    Fourth of July speech, 45–48,
        53
    Haiti, 74–80, 108, 109
Dubois, Laurent, 97, 102, 105
Du Bois, Shirley Graham, 61
Du Bois, W. E. B., 23, 57, 61, 62,
    129, 144

education, formal. *See* industrial
    educational; schools and schooling
Erickson, Ansley, 117
evolution, human. *See* human
    evolution
"eye color segregation" (classroom
    activity), 19–20

Fanon, Frantz, 72
Farmer, Ashley, 70–71
Federal Bureau of Investigation, 51,
    69
Fenwick, Leslie, 136, 139, 140
Fields, Barbara J., 18, 27, 41, 74,
    170n63
Fields, Karen, 4
Firmin, Anténor, 77, 78, 79
Fitzgerald, Robert, 128
Florida, 126–27
Foner, Eric, 55, 127, 128

Fourteenth Amendment, 120, 125
France
    Haiti and, 83–109 passim
    Louisiana sale, 101–2
Freedmen's Bureau, 124
"free people of color," 38–39, 40
French, Howard, 100
French Revolution, 89, 102, 111

Garvey, Marcus, 57, 58, 59, 62
genealogy, 35–41
Ghirardi, Bancroft, 77–78
Gibbs, Jonathan, 127
Gilmore, Ruth Wilson, 43
Glaude, Eddie, 151
Gonzalez, Johnhenry, 109
Gordon-Reed, Annette, 102,137
    reparations, 143
    France and Haiti, 106–7
Grant, Ulysses, 75, 130
Gray, William, 136
Great Britain. See Britain
Green, Hilary, 132–33, 134
Guinea, 65–66

Haiti
    "Ayiti," 83, 85, 105
    "Baby Doc" Duvalier, 71
    Frederick Douglass, 74–80
    Kreyòl, 92, 97, 102, 103
    as Macbeth setting, 146–47
    Môle Saint Nicolas, 77–79
    sugar and coffee, 87
    See also Haitian Revolution
Haitian immigrants (United States),
    41–42
Haitian Revolution, 8–9, 13, 81–111
The Haitians: A Decolonial History
    (Casimir), 89, 92–93, 103, 104,
    106
Hamer, Fannie Lou, 55–56, 61, 66,
    168n21

Hamilton, Alexander, 99, 100, 101–2
Hamilton, Charles, 71–72
Hampton Institute, 134, 179–80n60
Hannah-Jones, Nikole, 11–12, 33,
    155
Harlem Renaissance, 57, 147
Harrison, Benjamin, 76
Helps, David, 63–64
Hobsbawm, Eric, 170n63
Hoover, J. Edgar, 69
How Real Is Race? (Mukhopadhyay,
    Henze, and Moses), 25
human evolution, 23

indentured servitude, 28, 30
    colonial Virginia, 33, 35
individualism, 43
Indigenous people
    Haiti, 85
    North America, 30, 32, 38, 102
industrial education, 133–34,
    179–80n60
integration, racial. See racial
    integration
internationalism, 60–74 passim

James, C. L. R.: The Black Jacobins,
    87, 88, 92, 93
Jefferson, Thomas, 8, 53, 54–55, 91,
    98–101 passim
Jim Crow (racial segregation), 50, 52,
    66, 67, 121, 126
    in education, 119–20, 129, 137,
        138, 142
    See also Brown v. Board of
        Education; civil rights
        movement
Johnson, Andrew, 125
Johnson, Anthony, 29, 33
Johnson, James Weldon: "Lift Every
    Voice and Sing," 136
Johnson, Lyndon, 66, 67

Justice Department. *See* US
    Department of Justice

Kelley, Robin D. G., 5, 116
King, Martin Luther, Jr., 7, 51,
    55–56, 61, 62, 138, 141
Kochiyama, Yuri, 117–18
Kongos, 89
Ku Klux Klan, 129–30

labor unions. *See* unions
Lewis, John, 61, 65
libraries, 147. *See also* Schomburg
    Center for Research in Black
    Culture
"Lift Every Voice and Sing" (Johnson),
    156
Little, Earl, 58
Litwack, Leon, 132
Louisiana during Reconstruction,
    124, 127, 128, 132
Louisiana Purchase, 101–2
L'Ouverture, Toussaint, 93–101
    passim
Love, Bettina, 144
Lowndes County Freedom
    Organization. *See* Black Panther
    Party (Alabama)
loyalty, national. *See* national loyalty
    and disloyalty
lynching, 129–30

Madison, James, 99
Malcolm X, 2, 7, 57–62, 64–65, 73
    "The Ballot or the Bullet," 58–59
    international travel, 60–61
    Kochiyama relations, 117
Mallory, Mae, 142
Matthewson, Timothy, 100
melanin, 24
Mignolo, Walter, 103
Miller, George M., 114

Miller, Orisha "Bill," 146–47
Môle Saint Nicolas, Haiti, 77–79
Monroe, James, 84
Moore, Audley, 64, 70, 73
Morgan, Edmund, 53
"mulatto" (label), 40
Murch, Donna, 116, 117

Napoleon I, emperor of the French,
    95, 100–101
National Association for the
    Advancement of Colored People
    (NAACP), 63, 67
Nation of Islam (NOI), 56, 57, 58,
    60, 61
nations, 6–7, 24, 74
    Haiti, 86
    national loyalty and disloyalty,
        7, 49–53 passim, 73, 74
    national superiority, 9, 10, 121,
        152–53
    national unity, 51–52
Naturalization Act of 1790, 16
New Orleans
    Reconstruction, 128, 132
Newton, Huey, 68, 115, 116
New York City
    Baldwin childhood, 146–47
    Black Panthers, 113–18, 142,
        143
    schools, 118, 141–42
New York City Civil Rights History
    Project, 142–43
New York Public Library, 3, 11, 92,
    118, 147. *See also* Schomburg
    Center for Research in Black
    Culture
Nickens family, 38
Nkrumah, Kwame, 61
North Carolina, 38–41
    Reconstruction, 125

Obama, Barack, 7, 8
Ogé, Vincent, 93
Organization of African Unity
   (OAU), 64, 169n37

Pan-Africanism, 57, 61, 70
patriotism, 6–7, 53, 73, 74
Patterson, William, 63
Perry, Imani, 136
Plessy, Homer, 17, 41
Plessy v. Ferguson, 17–18, 121
Poitier, Sidney, 61
Porter, Herman "Bill," 147
Prosper, Mamyrah. *See* Dougé-
   Prosper, Mamyrah
Prosser, Gabriel, 84
protests and demonstrations, 21, 62,
   139, 142
public employment, 50–51

race, 5, 15–44 passim
   Haiti, 85, 105
racial integration
   Malcolm X view, 60
   MLK view, 138
   schools, 127, 128, 132, 137–42
      passim
   See also desegregation
racial passing, 41
racial profiling, 22 racial segregation.
   See Jim Crow (racial segregation)
racism, relationship to, 35. *See also*
   Blackness; whiteness
Randolph, A. Philip, 62
rape, 31, 35
Reconstruction, 9, 13, 55, 119–34
   passim, 144
Reconstruction Act of 1867, 125
reparations, 51, 70, 106, 131,
   143–44, 167n12
Republican Party
   Reconstruction, 125–31 passim

Rickford, Russell, 71
Robeson, Paul, 63
Robeson, Paul, Jr., 47, 63

Saint Domingue (French colony),
   81–103 passim
Schomburg Center for Research in
   Black Culture, 3, 4, 11, 81, 82,
   113–14, 117, 118
schools and schooling, 3, 4, 19–22,
   115–44 passim, 150–53
   standardized testing, 148–49
   *See also Brown v. Board of
      Education*
Schuller, Mark, 110
Seale, Bobby, 68, 115, 116
segregation. *See* Jim Crow (racial
   segregation)
settlers. *See* colonial settlers
Shaler, Nathaniel, 133
sickle-cell anemia, 25
skin color, 23–26 passim, 40
   as slave brand, 30
   See also Blackness; whiteness
slavery, 8, 36, 38, 52–54 passim
   abolition, 82, 94, 95
   colonial Virginia, 27–32 passim
   Haiti, 83–90 passim
   racial identity and, 17
   reparations, 51
   slave uprisings, 84
SNCC. *See* Student Nonviolent
   Coordinating Committee (SNCC)
South Carolina, 54, 81
   Denmark Vesey, 84
   Reconstruction, 126, 127, 128
Soviet Union, 60, 72–73, 121
Spain
   Haiti and, 83, 94, 101
Stern, Walter, 128

Student Nonviolent Coordinating Committee (SNCC), 64–69 passim, 73
suffrage. See voting rights
Supreme Court, US. See US Supreme Court

Táiwò, Olúfẹ́mi, 154
Texas
    Reconstruction, 127, 130
Theoharis, Jeanne, 143
Thirteenth Amendment, 125
Thornton, John, 89
tobacco production, colonial-era, 27, 28
Trouillot, Michel-Rolph, 96–97, 102, 111
Ture, Kwame (Stokely Carmichael), 61, 71–72
Tuskegee Institute, 4, 134, 138, 179–80n60

Ulysse, Gina Athena, 108
unions, 57
United Nations, 62–63, 69, 73
Universal Negro Improvement Association (UNIA), 56, 57, 58
US Civil War. See Civil War
US Constitution, 52–53, 137. See also Fourteenth Amendment; Thirteenth Amendment
US Department of Justice, 130
US Navy, 76, 101
USSR. See Soviet Union
US Supreme Court
    Brown, 10, 119–21, 134, 135, 138, 144
    Edward White, 130
    Plessy, 17–18, 121

Valdés, Vanessa, 92
Vastey, Pompée-Valentin, baron de, 88, 110–11
Vesey, Denmark, 84
Vietnam War, 66–67
Virginia
    colonial era, 27–35 passim
vitamin D deficiency, 24
Voices of a People's History of the United States, 2, 46–48
voting rights, 33, 54, 66, 126

Washington, Booker T., 97, 123–25, 134
Washington, George, 99, 100
Weaver family, 39–40
"We Charge Genocide," 63
Wells, Ida B., 55–56, 62
White, Edward, 130
"White Lives Matter," 42
whiteness, 17–18, 26, 40
    citizenship and, 16
    Haiti, 105
Wilkerson, Isabel, 6
Wilkins, Roy, 67
Williams, Heather, 122
Woodward, C. Vann, 52
Worth, Jonathan, 125
Wyatt family, 39, 40

X, Malcolm. See Malcolm X

Young, Whitney, 62, 66
Younge, Sammy, Jr., 66–67

Zinn, Howard
    Voices of a People's History of the United States, 2, 46–48

About Haymarket Books

Haymarket Books is a radical, independent, nonprofit book publisher based in Chicago. Our mission is to publish books that contribute to struggles for social and economic justice. We strive to make our books a vibrant and organic part of social movements and the education and development of a critical, engaged, and internationalist left.

We take inspiration and courage from our namesakes, the Haymarket Martyrs, who gave their lives fighting for a better world. Their 1886 struggle for the eight-hour day—which gave us May Day, the international workers' holiday—reminds workers around the world that ordinary people can organize and struggle for their own liberation. These struggles—against oppression, exploitation, environmental devastation, and war—continue today across the globe.

Since our founding in 2001, Haymarket has published more than nine hundred titles. Radically independent, we seek to drive a wedge into the risk-averse world of corporate book publishing. Our authors include Angela Y. Davis, Arundhati Roy, Keeanga-Yamahtta Taylor, Eve L. Ewing, aja monet, Mariame Kaba, Naomi Klein, Rebecca Solnit, Mohammed El-Kurd, José Olivarez, Noam Chomsky, Winona LaDuke, Robyn

Maynard, Leanne Betasamosake Simpson, Howard Zinn, Mike Davis, Marc Lamont Hill, Dave Zirin, Astra Taylor, and Amy Goodman, among many other leading writers of our time. We are also the trade publishers of the acclaimed Historical Materialism Book Series.

Haymarket also manages a vibrant community organizing and event space in Chicago, Haymarket House, the popular Haymarket Books Live event series and podcast, and the annual Socialism Conference.